B-52 STRATOFORTRESS VS SA-2 "GUIDELINE" SAM

Vietnam 1972–73

PETER E. DAVIES

OSPREY
Bloomsbury Publishing Plc
PO Box 883, Oxford, OX1 9PL, UK
1385 Broadway, 5th Floor, New York, NY 10018, USA
E-mail: info@ospreypublishing.com
www.ospreypublishing.com

OSPREY is a trademark of Osprey Publishing Ltd

First published in Great Britain in 2018

A catalogue record for this book is available from the British Library.

ISBN: PB 9781472823625; eBook 9781472823632; ePDF 9781472823656; XML 9781472823649

18 19 20 21 22 10 9 8 7 6 5 4 3 2 1

Edited by Tony Holmes
Cover artwork and battlescene by Gareth Hector
Three-views, cockpits, Engaging the Enemy, and armament scrap views by Jim Laurier
Maps and formation diagrams by Bounford.com
Index by Fionbar Lyons
Typeset by PDQ Digital Media Solutions, Bungay, UK
Printed in Hong Kong through World Print Ltd

Acknowledgments
I am grateful to the following for their assistance with this book – Col Dan Barry USAF (Ret), Col Don Blodgett USAF (Ret), Capt Danny Burnett USAF (Ret), Jim Cichocki USAF (Ret), Col John E. Frisby USAF (Ret), Gene Goss USAF (Ret), Dan Lapham USAF (Ret), Capt Robert Newton USAF (Ret), Nguyen Van Dinh, Nguyen Xuan Dai, Pham Truong Huy, Col Philip Rowe Jr USAF (Ret), Capt Ed Sandelius USAF (Ret), Lt Col Fred Sheffler USAF (Ret), Dr. István Toperczer, Lt Col Jim Tramel USAFRes (Ret), Maj Gordon Rees Williams USAF (Ret), Wayne C. Woods USAF (Ret). Particular thanks are due to Ken Kimmons USAF (Ret).

Cover artworks
B-52G 57-6496 "Quilt 03" from the 72nd Strategic Wing (Provisional) at Andersen AFB, Guam, was in a three-aircraft cell attacking Yen Vien, near Hanoi, on the night of December 20/21, 1972. The jet, with unmodified and faulty ECM that could only jam track-while-scan emissions, released its bombs as an SA-2 flashed past. Moments later the B-52 commenced its post-target turn, with two more SA-2s in pursuit. It was then hit as pilot Capt Terry Geloneck, on his first *Linebacker II* mission, hauled it into the headwind. Electronic Warfare Officer Capt Craig Paul and Radar-Navigator Capt Warren Spencer were killed, pressurization was lost and fuel and hydraulic systems were ruptured. The rest of the 456th BW crew from Beale AFB, California, successfully ejected and duly became PoWs. Capt Vlad Mancl, who was flying the B-52 immediately behind "Quilt 03," stated post-mission that he was amazed anyone had survived. (Cover artworks by Gareth Hector)

Title page
Six *Arc Light* crewmen with their flight baggage return from a mission in B-52F 57-0170 – probably its 32nd according to its scoreboard. After the initial *Arc Light*, SAC policy discouraged painting mission "scores" on the aircraft. *Arc Light* required a refueling rendezvous with a "Young Tiger" KC-135A about four hours after take-off from Andersen AFB, taking on 85,000–100,000lb of fuel. Andersen-based aircraft could end their mission at U-Tapao, subsequently flying up to eight more *Arc Light* sorties from the Thai base before returning to Guam. (USAF)

Contents

Introduction	4
Chronology	7
Design and Development	10
Technical Specifications	16
The Strategic Situation	25
The Combatants	36
Combat	52
Statistics and Analysis	70
Aftermath	76
Further Reading	79
Index	80

INTRODUCTION

Boeing's B-47 Stratojet, rolled out in September 1947, brought swept-wing, jet-powered technology to Strategic Air Command (SAC), although its range and payload limits made it a medium bomber. Gen Curtis LeMay's forceful leadership as SAC commander from October 1948 and increased Cold War tensions enabled the command to acquire more than 2,000 of these revolutionary aircraft. With six underwing General Electric J47 turbojet engines and fighter-like speed of Mach 0.86,

The Boeing B-47 Stratojet's J47 engines' slow acceleration and tight power margins left little room for error on take-off and landing, so rocket booster packs together with 10,000ft runways became necessary. The B-52's designers resolved many of the problems faced in conceiving this pioneering bomber, giving the new aircraft longer range, increased power, and better handling than the B-47. Radar jamming, which had been one the many jobs performed by the over-worked Stratojet co-pilot, now required a dedicated expert operator. (USAF)

the B-47 Stratojet was a key weapon in SAC's arsenal from 1951 until 1959, continuing as a reconnaissance platform after its successor, the Boeing B-52 Stratofortress, had become SAC's true heavy, long-range nuclear bomber.

B-52s were always expected to enter heavily defended airspace to deliver their weapons. Initially the threats to post-war bombers were from fighters and anti-aircraft fire, so designers focused on speed and altitude, devising heavy bombers capable of 550 knots above 48,000ft, beyond the reach of fighters. Nuclear weapons did not require precise aiming from that height, but by 1955 Russia was evolving surface-to-air missiles (SAMs) to intercept bombers at even higher altitudes. Soviet SAM designers, like their American counterparts who had introduced the SAM-A-7 Nike Ajax (the world's first operational SAM) in 1953, realized that a single nuclear bomber penetrating fighter defenses could cause untold havoc, so a network of radar-guided missiles offered optimum security from bombers and high-flying spy-planes. Flights by CIA Lockheed U-2s began in July 1956 but Soviet air defenses (PVO-Strany) were unable to destroy one with a SAM until May 1960.

A surviving SA-2 overlooks the wreckage of B-52D 56-0605 "Cobalt 01," felled by a SAM near Bac Ninh on December 27, 1972 and displayed in the Hanoi Museum of Victory over B-52. Of the six crewmen on board the bomber, only Maj Allen Johnson, the EWO for "Cobalt 01," and navigator 1Lt Bennie Fryer were killed. The latter did not eject from the aircraft, and it appears that he may have perished when the B-52 was hit, while Johnson almost certainly died in captivity. The Vietnam War saw SAC's most extensive combat operation and the largest number of ground-to-air missiles ever fired during a conflict. (via Dr. István Toperczer)

In Cuba, six Soviet ground-to-air missile regiments established 144 S-75 (SA-2) SAM launchers in the fall of 1962 in order to protect their secret nuclear intermediate-range ballistic missile sites. Only 90 miles off the US coast, these Russian-controlled weapons denied SAC its usual 15-minute reaction time to Soviet-based missiles, taking the world to the brink of nuclear warfare. After a US blockade of Soviet vessels delivering missiles, and an agreement to withdraw them, an impetuous Soviet commander defied orders and released three S-75s, destroying Maj Rudolph Anderson's U-2F as it flew over Cuba at 72,000ft. Col Don Blodgett flew one of the first B-52 24-hour alert missions during that tense time:

> I remember taking off the night that President Kennedy announced the blockade. After pulling up the gear and starting to climb I felt, "This is it. I will never see my wife again."

Anderson, who was killed in the incident, may not have seen the approaching SAMs due to cloud cover – a problem that was soon to plague US pilots over Vietnam. US Secretary of Defense Robert McNamara had assumed that the SA-2 sites were not yet operational, so no signals intelligence (SIGINT) cover was provided to detect hostile radar activity. The same authorities would underestimate the SA-2 in Vietnam too. After a Russian climbdown in Cuba, U-2 overflights continued over the northern Caribbean island nation. Although these were regularly tracked by the S-75's "Fruit Set" (later called "Fan Song") radars, effective electronic countermeasures (ECM) equipment to defeat them was initially forbidden from being installed in the U-2s in case it was captured should they crash or be shot down. The noise-jamming set used by SAC bombers was too heavy for the U-2, but System 12 ECM and a Sanders AN/ALQ-49 jammer derivative were eventually fitted. Much was learned about the SA-2's radar systems that would subsequently prove useful in protecting US aircraft, including the B-52.

A System 12-equipped CIA "Black Cat" U-2 flying in Chinese Nationalist Air Force colors was downed by three SA-2s in September 1962, this aircraft being the first of 12 similar losses over subsequent years.

Soviet SAMs forced SAC to change its Emergency War Order, and *Chrome Dome* nuclear alert missions moved from high altitude to ground-hugging routes below 500ft, where B-52s could hide from radar, missiles, and interceptors, including the MiG-21, designed specifically to intercept the Stratofortresses. Many of the B-52s' planned nuclear targets were Soviet missile sites. Capt Robert Newton recalled that grim scenario:

> Once you completed training you were assigned as a crew to a specific base and given a crew number in the order that you were assigned there. You became combat ready and you would be assigned a war mission and go on full alert. The first target our crew was assigned was the Kremlin. What a shocker for a 2nd Lieutenant!

During airborne alert, 24-hour Polar Zone flights bordering Soviet territory and involving several in-flight refueling sessions in radio silence, the primary job for a B-52 Electronic Warfare Officer (EWO) was monitoring occasional signals from Soviet long-range early-warning radars. Similar secure procedures were used for B-52 missions in Vietnam, where the bomber and SA-2 entered direct conflict for the first time, and that war's epic climax – the 11-day Operation *Linebacker II* attacks on the Hanoi and Haiphong areas of North Vietnam – resulted in prodigious use of SAMs, numerous losses of B-52s, and the first ECM war.

In October 1957 SAC's nuclear alert readiness posture was introduced, with a 15-minute notice "scramble" goal, later replaced by "minimum interval take-off" (MITO) mass launches. In 1959, to shorten the response time further, SAC began a 24-hour airborne alert with up to 12 B-52s – a costly precaution that was sustained until 1968. Here, a 92nd BW alert crew dash towards their B-52D (56-0590) at Fairchild AFB, Washington. (USAF)

CHRONOLOGY

1946

June — Boeing's Model 462, an enlarged B-29 derivative with six turboprop engines, is selected as a potential replacement for the Convair B-36. It is designated the XB-52.

1948

May — The evolved Boeing Model 464-40 has eight podded XJ40 turbojets. By October the Model 464-49 proposal includes eight J57 turbojets, a swept wing, and 330,000lb weight.

1951

January — Gen Curtis LeMay secures an order for 13 B-52As, delivered from April 1953.
A massive Berkut (Golden Eagle) defensive network using the S-25 SAM system is planned to defend Moscow.

The SA-2's ancestor, the S-25 (SA-1 "Guild") Berkut was a larger missile with a single liquid-fueled motor propelling it to around 60,000ft at Mach 2.5. Its warhead weighed up to 700lb. The Berkut entered service in 1956, and two concentric rings of launch sites were constructed around Moscow to tackle a mass raid by up to 1,000 B-52-type bombers. It was launched vertically from a fixed pad and guided by a B-20 "Yo Yo" track-while-scan radar. (Kapustin Yar Test Museum/Public domain)

1952

April 15 — YB-52 49-0231 completes its maiden flight. XB-52 49-0230 flies on October 2, 1952 and the B-52A on August 5, 1954.

1953

The Fakel S-75 Dvina missile (SA-2) is ordered to replace Almaz S-25 SAMs.

1955

January 25 — The first RB-52 flies, with deliveries of 50 B/RB-52Bs to the 93rd Bomb Wing at Castle AFB, California, commencing on June 29, 1955, followed by 35 B-52Cs.

1956

May 14 — The first of 170 B-52D flies, followed by 100 similar B-52Es (optimized for low-altitude operations) and 89 B-52Fs, completing Seattle's B-52 production by February 1959.

May 21 — B-52A 52-0013 delivers the first US thermonuclear weapon over Bikini Atoll.

July 4 — The first CIA U-2 spy flight over Russia is detected by Soviet radar, triggering development of the high-altitude 11D/S-75 missile.
The P-12 Yenisey ("Spoon Rest") surveillance radar for SAM sites enters Soviet service.

December 11 — The S-75 missile, with its P-12 radar, PRV-10 height-finder and RSNA-75 ("Fan Song") fire-control radar units, enters Soviet service.

1958

August 31 — The first B-52G flies (193 produced up to September 23, 1960). The TF33 turbofan-equipped B-52H (102 manufactured) appears in 1961. Both carry stand-off weapons such as GAM-77 Hound Dog. Early B-52s are equipped with AN/ALQ-27 multi-band jamming and Quail radar decoy missiles. 743 B-52s were produced by June 1962.
The improved S-75N (13D) *Desna* SAM enters Soviet production.

October — SA-75/V-750 missiles, supplied to China, make the first SAM kill; a ROCAF RB-57D reconnaissance aircraft.

1959

February 3 — The B-52G enters service with the 5th BW two days after retirement of the last B-36, thus making SAC an all-jet force.

1960

May 1 — Francis Gary Powers' *Grand Slam* U-2C is destroyed by S-75N missiles.

1962

Two Soviet PVO-Strany S-75 divisions are deployed to Cuba.
An improved S-75, the 20D guided by the upgraded Almaz RSN-75V ("Fan Song E") radar, enters PVO-Strany service.

October 27 — A CIA U-2F falls to SA-2s over Cuba.

1963

SAC's B-52 force comprises 38 Bomb Wings.

1965

February — Thirty B-52Fs deploy to the 3960th SW at Andersen AFB, Guam, flying the first Operation *Arc Light* mission against Viet Cong forces on June 18.

April — Soviet S-75 (SA-75MK Dvina/Fakel 11D) missile regiments deploy around Hanoi and are detected by US Navy aircraft.

July — A USAF F-4C Phantom II becomes the first Vietnam SA-2 casualty.
USAF/US Navy *Iron Hand* attacks on SA-2 sites begin and *Wild Weasel* ECM-equipped aircraft are developed.

1966

B-52Ds with increased *Big Belly* conventional bombing capability, tactical camouflage and Phase III ECM updates replace B-52Fs by April with the newly established 4133rd BW (Provisional) at Andersen AFB. Attacks on Laotian targets begin on April 11. A total of 5,000 B-52 sorties are flown by September 14.

September — B-52Ds are engaged by SA-2s but jam the missiles.
Soviet experts modify some Vietnamese "Fan Song Fs" with optical tracking.

1967

April — In Operation *Poker Dice*, B-52Ds deploy to U-Tapao Royal Thai Navy Air Base (RTNAB), Thailand.

1968

January — Kadena AB, Okinawa, briefly becomes the third Southeast Asian B-52D base for combat operations.
After the end of Operation *Rolling Thunder* in October, *Arc Light* close air-support missions against the Viet Cong in South Vietnam and neighboring Laos and Cambodia continue.

1969

The Soviet Union has in excess of 800 S-75 batteries and exports many more to Warsaw Pact nations.

1970 President Richard Nixon's draw-down of US forces in Southeast Asia ends B-52D operations at Kadena and Andersen AFBs by September. U-Tapao increases *Arc Light* missions against the Ho Chi Minh trail. Some SA-2 sites move to southern North Vietnam.

1971 North Vietnam is denied the improved S-75M2 Volkhov SAM system.

1972 Operation *Bullet Shot* deployments return B-52Ds to Andersen AFB after the North Vietnamese invasion of South Vietnam. *Bullet Shot III* adds 28 B-52Gs to Andersen's 43rd SW (Provisional). F-105G *Wild Weasel* aircraft deploy to Thailand, remaining until 1974.

April 15/16 Attacks near Vinh attract 35 SA-2s. Near Than Hoa, 50 SA-2s are launched and one B-52D is damaged during Operation *Freedom Train*.

May 10 Operation *Linebacker* begins. More than 2,500 *Arc Light* sorties prevent North Vietnam from taking the cities of Kontum and An Loc.

November 22 The first B-52D (55-0110) is lost to an SA-2.

December 18/21 Operation *Linebacker II* begins, hitting Hanoi with 321 B-52 sorties. Eight are lost to SA-2s (600 launches reported) and two seriously damaged.

December 21/24 Phase II of *Linebacker II* uses fewer sorties, all from U-Tapao. Some target SA-2 sites. Two B-52s lost.

December 26/29 Phase III of *Linebacker II* sees 120 B-52s launched and four lost to SA-2s. On December 28/29 B-52s hit SA-2 sites and storage.

December 30 *Linebacker II* ends, with 39 out of 95 SAM sites still active and 850 of the 7,658 missiles supplied still in storage.

B-52Gs receive *Rivet Ace* Phase VI ECM defensive avionics.

Hidden under camouflage netting, SAM troops and their Soviet PVO-Strany instructors pose with an SA-2 in May 1965. (via Dr. István Toperczer)

1973

January 3/4 B-52D 55-0056 becomes the last Vietnam Stratofortress lost to SAMs. *Arc Lights* over Cambodia cease on August 15, ending eight years of B-52 combat missions. The aircraft immediately return to nuclear deterrence.

DESIGN AND DEVELOPMENT

B-52A/G STRATOFORTRESS

The B-52 was conceived when six senior Boeing designers led by Ed Wells responded to proposals in October 1948 by Col Henry Warden, USAF Chief of Bomber Development, to replace turboprops in their Model 464 bomber project with the planned Pratt & Whitney J57 turbojet. A three-day design marathon resulted in the Model 464-49-0 with eight J57s, "podded" under a flexible wing, swept at 35 degrees, spanning 185ft and 4,000 sq ft in area. At twice the B-47's gross weight, with an airframe about two-thirds larger, its J57 engines developed up to 110,000lb total thrust.

Pratt & Whitney's first jet engine, the JT3A/J57 was, in propulsion expert Bill Gunston's opinion, "the most important post-war jet engine," and in January 1950 the first to develop over 10,000lb of thrust. Although it was the company's first production turbojet and designed for the B-52, it powered a generation of US military aircraft. Converted into a turbofan as the TF33, it provided improved power and fuel economy for the later B-52H.

Weight estimates for the new bomber were around 330,000lb and it could achieve speeds exceeding 490 knots with a 10,000lb bomb-load over a 2,660 nautical mile radius. The target altitude for the B-52 was 50,000ft, although control would be marginal at that height. Range could be extended by the Boeing KC-135 tankers that Gen LeMay had requested to replace SAC's fleet of piston-engined KC-97s.

The B-52 Stratofortress was ordered in February 1951 before it flew (in preference to Convair's similar YB-60), confirming LeMay's belief in the design, and the urgent need for the bomber after five years of design definition. For him, the Cold War was a real conflict. Production facilities and sub-contractors were arranged in great secrecy for the massive airframe components and work began on the aircraft's advanced avionics.

The pilots of the second RB-52B complete take-off with 98 percent power, 42psi oil pressure, and the eight throttles close to the fully open position. (Alamy)

Low-speed handling was improved by spoilers controlling both lift and bank and preventing the undesirable swept-wing phenomenon known as aileron reversal, caused by ailerons effectively warping the wing. The aircraft's 28ft-long bomb-bay was six feet wide – sufficiently large enough to house a full range of ordnance or (for the RB-52B/C) a pressurized reconnaissance pod. Although the tail surfaces were conventional, the horizontal stabilizer could be trimmed for limited rotation on take-off and flare on landing. The bicycle undercarriage used eight wheels on four struts, with two outrigger wheels protecting the wing-tips. Weight-saving pneumatic auxiliary systems were powered by engine bleed air, although the horizontal stabilizer, bomb-bay doors, spoilers, brakes, and undercarriage steering were hydraulic.

Construction of similar XB-52 and YB-52 prototypes progressed through 1951, and on March 15, 1952 test pilot Tex Johnson and his USAF equivalent Lt Col Guy Townsend made an uneventful first flight in YB-52 49-0231. B-52Cs and similar B-52Ds (with an MA-6A bombing/navigation system, uprated J57-P-29W engines and improved ECM) were produced at Boeing's Seattle and Wichita factories, these aircraft serving with 36 SAC wings from 1956.

The most visible changes for the B-52G were a shorter vertical tail and smaller 700-gallon, non-jettisonable external fuel tanks. New alloys enabled lighter wing construction, with more integrated flight control, hydraulic, and electrical systems making the B-52G more reliable, but also more vulnerable to combat damage than the B-52D because integral, non-self-sealing fuel tanks (adding 8,719 gallons of internal fuel and 30 percent more range) replaced self-sealing bladder-type containers. Conventional ailerons were deleted to save weight and roll control was provided by the seven comb-like spoilers, visible in this view of B-52G 58-0231, which formed airbrakes when raised together. (USAF)

B-52D

Boeing (Wichita) made all the B-52Gs – the most numerous variant – supplied to the USAF, this model having better ejection seats, improved bombing and navigation equipment, internal wing tanks, and fundamental design changes to save weight and structural stress in low-altitude turbulence. B-52Ds also required extensive structural modification to withstand low-altitude operational stresses. Empty weight for the B-52G was reduced and maintenance man-hours were cut by a quarter. The gunner was moved from the fuselage tail-end to more comfortable conditions in the main cabin, being sat alongside the EWO and operating his guns remotely. Deletion of his pressurized tail compartment saved 1,000lb of weight, but removed a valuable rearward observation point. Cockpit re-design was an advantage according to Maj Rees Williams:

> The B-52G had better air conditioning and the cabin was more comfortable at high altitudes and low power settings.

OPPOSITE
B-52D 56-0629, the penultimate D-model built, flew many *Arc Light* and *Linebacker* missions with the 428th SW from U-Tapao RTNAB. The wing, which controlled the B-52Ds of the 364th and 365th BS(P)s, became the 307th SW after 1970, remaining at U-Tapao until June 1975. On its retirement, this aircraft, accepted for SAC service in October 1957, became an exhibit in the Global Air Power Museum at Barksdale AFB, Louisiana.

S-75 DVINA (NATO CODENAME SA-2 "GUIDELINE")

Design of the S-75 semi-mobile system began in 1953, with work being undertaken by the new Almaz design bureau headed by Pyotr Grushin. He assisted with the development of the S-25 Berkut system involving 60 missile sites operated by 56 regiments charged with protecting Moscow from bombers like the B-52. Premier Joseph Stalin saw the B-52 as the main threat to the USSR, although it would be almost 20 years before the S-75 would actually be used against it.

Almaz designed two versions of the S-75, the SA-75N Dvina (entering service in 1957) using low-frequency (ten-centimeter) N-band radars and the S-75N Desna (available from 1969) operating on V-band at the higher six-centimeter wavelength. Both used the V-750 two-stage missile fired from single-rail launchers and guided by an Almaz RSNA-75 "Fan Song" fire-control radar after initial target detection and

SA-75MK Dvina missiles were supplied to Egypt from 1965, with 27 batteries being used in two wars with Israel. Here, an SM-63 launcher is about to be re-loaded with a Dvina from a PRB-11B trans-loader and ZiL-157KV tractor unit. Although the Israeli Defense Force Air Force conceded 102 aircraft losses between 1967 and 1973, only two were attributed to SA-75s largely due to the Israelis' effective use of US-supplied ECM pods. (DoD)

tracking, typically by a P-12 "Spoon Rest" search radar and a PRV-11 "Side Net" height-finding radar. The additional radars were needed as the "Fan Song's" radar beam covered only a ten-degree sector.

A missile battalion site housed six SM-63-1 launchers, a low-frequency van-mounted P-12 Yenisei "Spoon Rest-A" radar with a six-element Yagi-Uda narrow band-width directional antenna and a 300-nautical-mile range, a "Fan Song" missile guidance radar and, in some cases, an obsolescent van-mounted P-10 "Knife Rest" height-finding radar, although height information often came via a land-line. "Spoon Rest" needed two ZiL vehicles for the antenna and its radar instruments. Battalion HQ also operated a van-mounted P-15 "Flat Face" UHF-band search-and-track radar and a PRV-11 "Side Net" height-finding radar. DES-75 diesel-powered electricity-generating vehicles and ATS-59 tractors were also required. Other equipment for "Fan Song," including analogue tracking computers, radar processors, and uplink transmitters, was housed in an "AV" cabin. All were road transportable for rapid relocation.

SA-2 "Guideline"

An SA-2 on its PR-11AM transporter-loader, towed by a ZiL-151 6x6 tractor powered by a 92hp six-cylinder engine. The tractor, based on a standard lorry unit produced by ZiS/ZiL, Russia's main provider of military vehicles, could negotiate very rough terrain. The 90-inch-wide semi-trailer transporter unit, designed by TsKB-34, included a rail from which the 34.5ft SA-2 could be slid by two electric motors directly onto its SM-63-1 launcher.

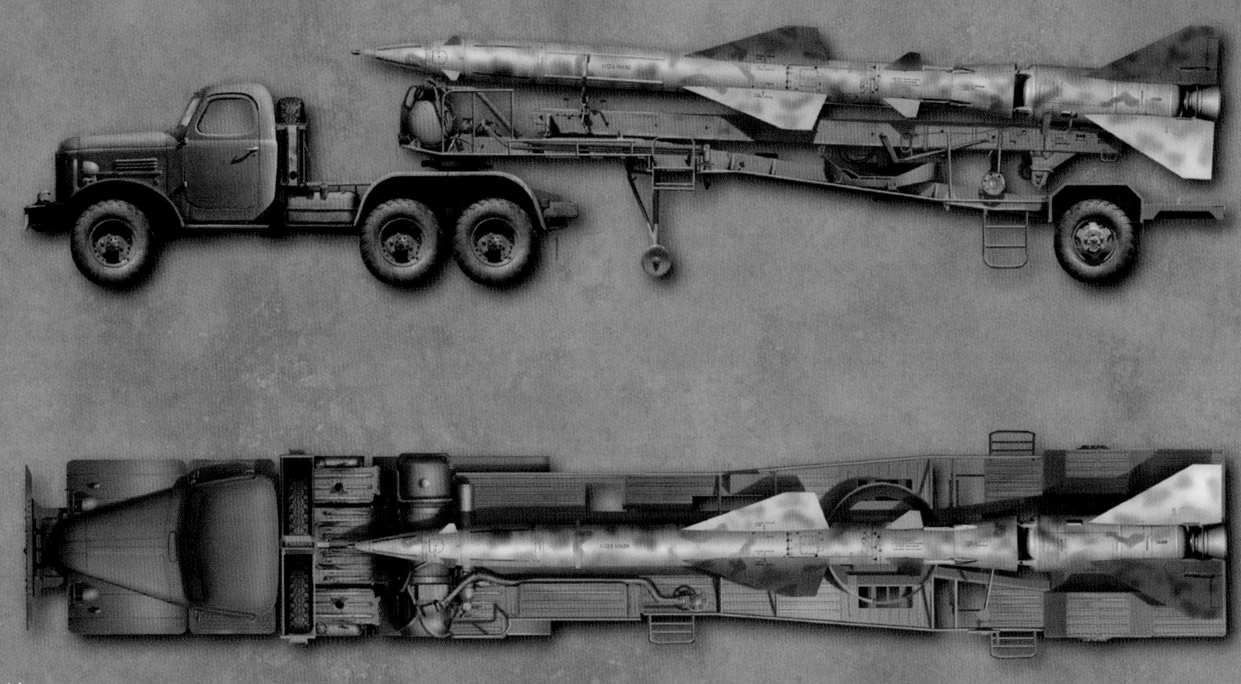

Some early SA-2s were used in the 1965 Indo-Pakistan War while Russia proceeded with the faster, longer-ranging S-75 Volkhov system. The later Model 17D used a ramjet instead of a liquid-fuel rocket motor and led to the improved Fakel 19D and 22D ramjet variants.

LEFT

A rear view of a RSNA-75 "Fan Song B," which was the standard 1965 Soviet model, supplemented by RSN-75V2 "Fan Song F" from 1968 with a "bird house" cabin above the horizontal antenna in which two seated operators could track and guide an SA-2 optically in daylight if enemy jamming was too intense. "Fan Song E" had two additional parabolic antennas above its horizontal Lewis scanner to counter ECM. (DoD)

LEFT

North Vietnamese missile troops prepare a weapon for launching. Clouds of red-orange smoke and dust were visible warnings of an SA-2/S-75 launch by day, but the yellow and white glare of the sustainer motors during night-time launches was often hidden by heavy cloud bases throughout most of *Linebacker II*. By the late 1960s the USSR had around 1,000 SA-2 sites, and many others were established in Warsaw Pact countries. China developed its own license-built version, the HQ-2, including a missile mounted on a tracked vehicle launcher. (via Dr. István Toperczer)

TECHNICAL SPECIFICATION

Groundcrew brave the fierce mid-day sun to work on the J57-P-29W engines of B-52D 56-0609 during Operation *Linebacker II* at U-Tapao. Taking off from Andersen AFB, Guam, heavily laden B-52Ds usually struggled in the high temperatures and humidity. Former pilot Maj Rees Williams remembered that "many missions were flown on seven engines and some on six. Loss of two engines on take-off from Guam posed a real problem, and it happened several times." (USAF)

B-52 STRATOFORTRESS

The B-52 was big in every sense of the word, and the key to both its effectiveness as a weapon of war and its longevity was the aircraft's wing structure. It could support eight engines, external fuel tanks (holding 3,000 gallons as drop-tanks on the C- to F-models) and inboard ordnance pylons – the latter were deleted on the B-52E. Massive four-segment Fowler flaps extended over 797sq ft when lowered at 35 degrees. No fewer than ten hydraulic packs were required to operate the flaps, as well as the complex undercarriage, utility systems, and remaining flying surfaces.

The bicycle undercarriage configuration, wing incidence, and the lift imparted by the huge tailplane caused a slightly nose-low take-off and climb position without conventional rotation. A unique "crosswind crab" facility adjusted the undercarriage orientation by 20 degrees to each side so that the aircraft could land with the wheels aligned to the runway, increasing its crosswind limits to 43 knots. It also enabled sideways taxiing

into a parking space. Outrigger undercarriage units ("pilot training wheels") dictated a minimum 300ft runway width. A 44ft-diameter drag 'chute deployed in four seconds on touchdown.

B-52Ds had a complex, co-pilot operated electrical panel with three switches for each of four generators and a very high pressure turbine-driven pneumatic system from which leaking super-heated air could cause major damage. Whereas the B-52D system supplied overall pneumatic power from any engine, a lost engine in a B-52G also denied electrical or hydraulic power to one of six systems associated with it. The fuel system required constant monitoring to preserve the center of gravity and ensure continuous supply to each engine. B-52Ds also introduced the AN/ASQ-38 Offensive Weapons System which, although a great advance on the previous MA-6A bombing/navigation system was, "a real Pandora's Box of electro/mechanical and electronic components, and it was not easy to maintain" according to former B-52 technician, Dan Lapham. "It was so tough to work on that it took years for most guys to get a handle on it. Many never really did."

An MD-3 external unit powered up the eight turbine-driven J57 starters. Black powder cartridges could start engine Nos 2 and 8, with compressed air from those engines starting the others to meet the 15-minute nuclear alert deadline, but cartridges were unreliable and usually avoided. An injection system sprayed 300 gallons of water into the engine inlets, where it vaporized, creating denser, oxygen-rich air for 110 seconds of extra take-off thrust at 86 percent power and 70 knots. In B-52Gs, another 1,200lb of water added two minutes of boosted thrust, totaling 110,000lb.

With conventional weapons the B-52D's maximum release speed was usually 350 knots indicated air speed at 30,000–32,000ft, giving a bombing pattern up to a mile long and 300ft wide with craters 30ft to 150ft apart, depending on airspeed. The rapid transfer of B-52Gs to Southeast Asia for *Linebacker II* precluded *Big Belly* modifications to increase their internal bomb-load, limiting their ordnance to 27 M117 750lb bombs – roughly a third of a B-52D's load.

ABOVE LEFT
From December 1965 the Big Belly/Sun Bath high-density bomb-load modifications enabled B-52Ds to carry 84 Mk 82 or 42 M117 (seen here) clip-mounted bombs internally and 24 M117s on underwing racks, totaling around 60,000lb. (USAF)

ABOVE RIGHT
A loaded "clip" of 500lb Mk 82 general purpose bombs, fuzed and ready to load into B-52D's belly at a U-Tapao. The bomb-bay doors could be swung upwards to allow the bomb-loading "jammer" access to the bay. With so many bombs falling in 10–20 seconds, collisions often occurred, causing some to go off course. They took about 2.5 minutes to hit the ground from 35,000ft, aimed with the AN/ASQ-48 bombing/navigation system. Guam used pre-loaded clips of bombs in 1972 while Andersen hand-loaded individually. *Arc Light* B-52s sometimes carried 24 1,000lb bombs internally. (USAF)

BLACK BOXES VERSUS SAMS

In 1953 the USA began programs to combat ground-to-air missiles, although progress was slow before the Vietnam conflict. A B-52's four M3 0.50-caliber tail guns

B-52G CUTAWAY

1. Command deck – pilot and co-pilot
2. Radar equipment
3. Navigators' compartment
4. Crew bunk and avionics rack
5. EWO and gunner's station
6. Forward fuel cells
7. Wing center fuel tanks
8. Aft fuel cells
9. Hydraulic reservoir
10. Rear ECM equipment bays
11. Brake parachute
12. AN/ASG-15 radome
13. AN/APR-25 radome
14. M3 0.50-caliber machine guns (x4)
15. Ammunition boxes and feed chutes
16. Aft ECM equipment bay
17. Liquid oxygen converter
18. Strike camera bay
19. Undercarriage bays
20. Bomb-bay and M117 bombs
21. Forward ECM bay
22. Avionics compartments

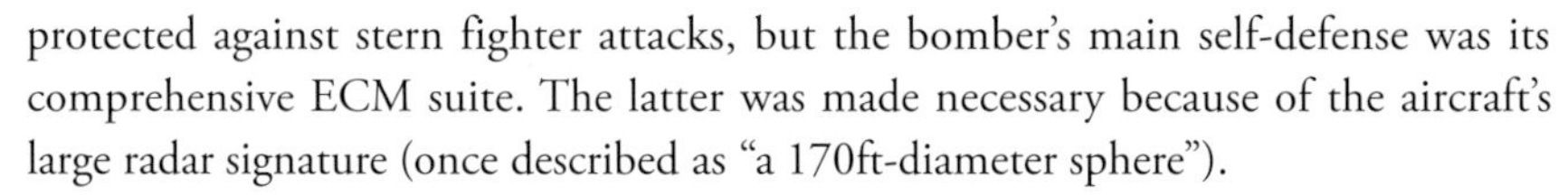

protected against stern fighter attacks, but the bomber's main self-defense was its comprehensive ECM suite. The latter was made necessary because of the aircraft's large radar signature (once described as "a 170ft-diameter sphere").

Equipment to jam and deceive enemy target-tracking radars soon comprised a substantial portion of the aircraft's empty weight. B-52s were among the earliest aircraft with an assigned EWO (requiring an extensive recruitment effort), although his ECM suite initially included only basic noise jammers such as the AN/APT-1 and AN/APT-5, together with AN/APR-14 and AN/APR-9 receivers to interpret radar emissions. The EWO's craft originated in World War II and Allied jamming of German radio communications, and as the electronic warfare threat scenario developed during the 1960s his importance increased.

Four M3 0.50-caliber machine guns comprised the defensive armament of most B-52s prior to the B-52H. Each gun fired 750 rounds per minute, drawing belted ammunition from a tank that was winched up into the rear fuselage. (USAF)

Up to five AN/ALT-6B jammers were progressively installed. AN/ALE-1 chaff dispensers were fitted on either side of the fuselage below the vertical tail, with two bins each holding 600lb of chaff. As enemy radars became more sophisticated, with shifting frequencies to defeat jamming, the EWO's job became more complex. Spot jamming could be directed at a single radar signal, barrage jamming covered a range of hostile emissions and sweep jamming automatically shifted the jamming over numerous frequencies, but reduced the power available to block each signal.

Although the AN/ALQ-27 ECM system was originally planned for the B-52D, its estimated $1bn costs caused cancelation. It was replaced by the "Big Four" program in three phases of the Quick Reaction Capability system, culminating in Phase III with some AN/ALQ-27 features by 1963. This included a General Electric AN/ALR-18 automatic set-on receiver, two AN/ALT-15H

high-band jamming sets and one AN/ALT-15L low-band jammer. Five General Electric Modulated AN/ALT-6B continuous-wave E/F-band jamming transmitters and two AN/ALT-13(V) barrage jammers countered "Fan Song" radar azimuth, elevation beams, and missile downlinks. Modified B-52Gs had three modulated AN/ALT-22 track-while-scan beacon jammers.

Phase IV, installed from 1964 to 1966, improved warning and jamming capability to prepare the B-52D/F for "Fan Songs" in Vietnam. An AN/ALT-16 barrage-jammer, a Tasker AN/ALR-20 panoramic countermeasures receiving set and an Itek AN/APR-25 radar homing and warning receiver were added. Six Dynalectron AN/ALE-20 flare dispensers held 96 pyrotechnics. Chaff was dispensed from eight Lundy AN/ALE-24s and two AN/ALE-25s, with 1,125 chaff bundles in the wings as single packets or streamed. Phase IV equipment weighed up to 6,000lb (each AN/ALT-13 weighed 150lb), but Vietnam experience would justify this costly re-fit.

The first SAM launch at a the B-52 in 1967 triggered *Rivet Rambler* Phase V for B-52Ds and about half of the B-52Gs from 1967 to 1969. It added three Northrop AN/ALT-32L low-band pulse jammers, with two more powerful AN/ALT-32H high-band jammers to replace the AN/ALT-15 units. There were six Hallicrafters AN/ALT-28 noise jammers, which were more powerful than the AN/ALT-13(V)s, and two Hallicrafters AN/ALT-16 D-band noise barrage-jammers. An AN/ALT-18 dealt with MiG airborne radars. Some B-52Gs could carry Westinghouse's AN/ALQ-119(V) ECM pod on an external pylon. B-52Gs that lacked *Rivet Rambler* ECM upgrades had Phase III AN/ALT-6B jammers that were less powerful than the B-52D's AN/ALT-22s.

The B-52G retained M3 guns but removal of the gunner's compartment required the installation of a TV camera above the weapons, replaced in later G-models by the AN/ALQ-117's radome with an AN/ASG-15 search antenna projecting above it. (Author's Collection)

B-52D/G Specifications (B-52G in brackets)	
Dimensions	
Length	156.58ft (157.6ft)
Wingspan	185ft
Tailplane	span 52ft
Height	48.25ft (40.67ft)
Wing area	4,000 sq ft
Height from ground to top of fuselage	17.45ft
Undercarriage track between outriggers	148.45ft
Weights	
Empty	170,126lb (158,737lb)
Max take-off*	450,000lb (488,000lb)
*often exceeded by up to 20,000lb to allow for fuel and water consumption before lift-off.	
Performance	
Max speed	551 knots at 20,000ft
Typical combat maximum speed	450–470 knots
Service ceiling	55,000ft with pressure suits for the crew or, in Vietnam, 46,200ft (46,000ft)
Combat radius	3,305 nautical miles (3,785 nautical miles)
Ferry range	6,820 nautical miles (7,730 nautical miles)
Powerplant	(B-52D) eight Pratt & Whitney J57-P-19W or J57-P-29W axial flow turbojets developing 12,100lb "wet" thrust (with mineralized water injection) (B-52F/G) eight J-57-P-43WB developing 13,750lb "wet" thrust
Fuel capacity	B-52D 41,550 US gal, B-52G 47,975 US gal
Armament	four M3 0.50-caliber machine guns with 600 rounds and MD-9 fire-control system (Avco-Crosley AN/ASG-15 in B-52G)

OPPOSITE
A camouflaged SA-2 (or 11D, the standard S-75 export model) on its SM-63-1 launcher. Difficulty in locating and attacking SAM sites, due to their mobility and camouflage, during their first six months of operations brought a new emphasis on defeating them through electronic methods by detecting and jamming their command frequencies. Jamming blunted the SA-2's automatic guidance mode except when B-52s were turning steeply, and if a whole cell turned simultaneously close to a SAM site, it had virtually no protection for up to 20 seconds, allowing a change to automatic lock-on by a manually guided missile that was already airborne. (via Dr. István Toperczer)

S-75 (SA-2 "GUIDELINE" MOD 0)

Designated the V-750 (sometimes V-75) Dvina in the Soviet Union, the missile is better known in the West as the S-75 or by its NATO name, SA-2 "Guideline" Mod 0. Evolved from the 1944 German *Wasserfall* missile concept, the weapon was designed to protect the strategic and population centers of Russia, but it soon became the primary and longest-serving air defense missile offered to the Soviet Union's allies too. Several variants were developed, including the short-lived experimental V-753 that was to be fired from an eight-round magazine aboard *Sverdlov*-Class cruisers. Developed quickly in the mid-1950s, the missile was designed to intercept targets at medium to high altitude. Its performance against aircraft below 3,000ft was poor.

The first ground-to-air missile to be used in combat, the SA-2 received its first five seconds of thrust from a Kartukov PRD-18 booster section with 14 NMF-2 solid propellant tubes and four large stabilizing fins. During that time the missile was unmaneuverable. Its main 94lb Isayev S2.711V1 sustainer rocket motor then drove the SA-2 to Mach 3 using hypergolic liquid propellant made from TG-02 (roughly equal proportions of isometric xylidine and triethylamine, with 1.5 percent diethylamine), with AK-20F fuming nitric acid as oxidizer. A turbopump fed these chemicals to the motor for 22 seconds, and after burn-out the missile rapidly lost speed and maneuverability. This hazardous brew was pumped into the missile by technicians (initially Soviet troops) wearing extensive protective clothing. Later versions of the S-75 such as the 20D (S-75M2) used safer kerosene/Trikresol fuel.

A compressed air tank pressurized the fuel system and powered the small steering fins ahead of the motor section. A 5E11 Schmel (or 5E29) radio proximity fuze was installed, linked to external strip antennas on the body or radome with a back-up impact fuze.

Steering fins gave limited maneuverability while the missile was climbing towards a non-maneuvering target. After motor burn-out any maneuvering quickly sapped its energy. Programed via a beacon in the missile's tail, a proximity fuze detonated the warhead within 210ft of the target, spraying 8,000 fragmented metal sections at 7,000ft per minute over an 800ft radius at an altitude of 35,000ft. Shrapnel projected forward conically to hit targets ahead of its flight-path and outwards in a circle from the rear of the warhead for targets abeam the missile, with a lethal radius of about 400ft. In darkness, the explosion created blue and orange cloud around the missile. B-52 hydraulics, pneumatic systems, and engines were extremely vulnerable to shrapnel.

Each missile had an AP-75 autopilot module linked to an FR-15Yu UHF uplink command receiver (transponder), a battery and transducer. The FR-15Yu used two wave-forms to provide climb/dive or turn commands to the steering fins. Two wave-forms armed and programmed the proximity fuze. The modules had relevant frequencies and codes

A "Fan Song B" preserved in Hanoi, with the Vietnamese slogan "Nothing is more precious than independence and freedom" in yellow on its horizontal antenna. North Vietnam's radars operated in the frequency spectrum from A-band (up to 250MHz) to J-band (from 10,000–20,000 MHz), with SAM radars working around the middle of that range. "Fan Song A/B" worked in the E/F-bands. (via Dr. István Toperczer)

SA-2 CUTAWAY

1. Radio proximity fuze transmit antenna
2. FR-15 Shmel radio proximity fuze
3. V-88 warhead
4. Radio proximity fuze receive antenna
5. AK-20F oxidizer melange tank
6. TG-02 propellant tank
7. Compressed air tank
8. AP-75 autopilot module
9. FR-15Yu command link module
10. Battery
11. Transducer
12. Cruciform controls
13. OT-155 Isonate turbopump gas-generator propellant tank
14. Isayev S2.711 liquid propellant sustainer powerplant
15. Adapter fairing
16. PRD-18 boost powerplant with 14 tubes of NMF-2 propellant

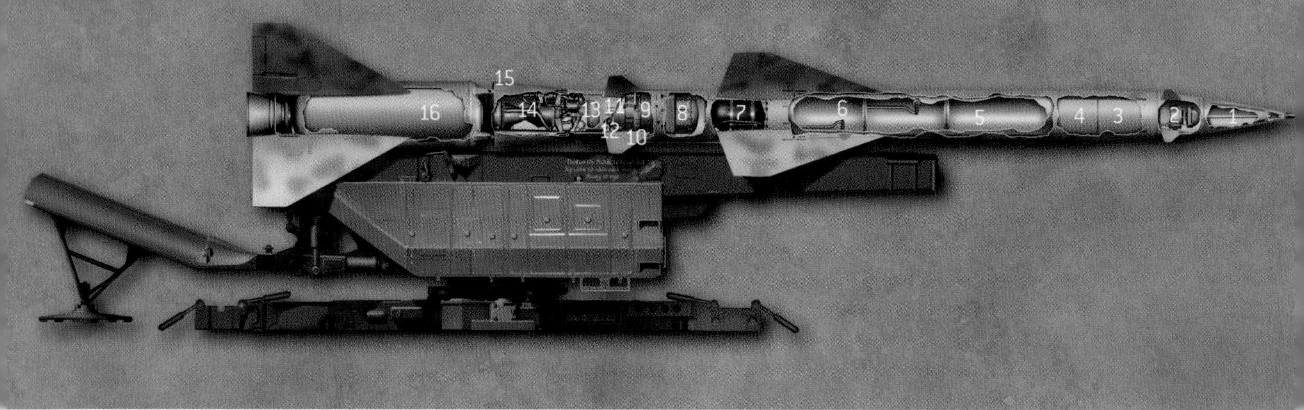

programmed into them to link them to a particular launch site's command equipment. A downlink radar beacon transmitted the missile's position into the "Fan Song." Inbound American strike forces were detected initially by some of North Vietnam's 200 radar sites, including three main ground-control interception sites, all linked by land-lines to airfields, missile, and anti-aircraft artillery (AAA) sites. A missile launch was initiated by pressing the "Fan Song's" Target Transmitter button to activate the radar.

SA-2 launchers sheltered in revetments of about 40ft diameter, roughly 200ft apart, in a flower-shaped pattern, with access roads to each revetment for the lengthy missile transporters. In the ideal Soviet scenario most support vans apart from "Fan Song" were in protective trenches, but in North Vietnam they were often camouflaged in the open for speedy transit. Mobile "commando" battalions with forward-based missiles transported up to three launchers and a "Fan Song" to an "ambush" site position

A line-up of trans-loader units from the 261st "Thang Long" Missile Regiment before they were positioned to defend Hanoi. Commanded by Tran Huu Lao, the regiment included four of the most successful battalions of the *Linebacker* period, defending the northeastern approaches to Hanoi and claiming eight of the 15 B-52 losses. Like the other battalions, their main problem was lack of assembled missiles. (via Dr. István Toperczer)

before rapidly relocating, with consequent attrition of delicate electronic components, to avoid air attack. They often had to set up their launchers on unsuitably soft terrain, distorting the SM-63-1 launch rails.

In December 1972 SAC expected to face 32 SAM battalions in four air defense divisions covering six areas of North Vietnam. They protected Hanoi, Haiphong and the main railway into China, and were supported by nine technical battalions. There were also SAM-defended areas to the south around Than Hao, Dong Hoi, and Vinh. Reconnaissance detected around 2,300 SA-2s and 200 launchers, with more in storage. SAM sites were allocated numbers (e.g. VN-243) based on the order of their discovery, although many were periodically unoccupied in a constantly-changing pattern. Initially, batteries stayed at a site for three or four days before moving in a ten-vehicle convoy to another location by night in a regular sequence that involved periods of maintenance or training. The demands of *Linebacker II* made regular movements to avoid air attack more difficult. Sites were frequently placed in civilian areas for protection from air strikes.

ALMAZ RSN-75V2 "FAN SONG F"

Although it was reluctant to supply North Vietnam with its most advanced military equipment, the Soviet Union did provide the RSN-75V2 version of the "Fan Song" unit. Virtually identical in layout to the original SNR-75M "Fan Song B" Missile Control Radar, the RSN-75V2 had an additional "bird house" structure above its horizontal Lewis "trough" scanner. This modification was first carried out by Soviet advisors in North Vietnam during September 1966. Two seated operators within the "bird house" could track and guide an SA-2 optically in daylight if enemy jamming was too intense to allow the "Fan Song's" radar to be employed effectively.

S-75MK Dvina (SA-2) System Specifications	
Dimensions	
Total weight	5,041lb
Length	34.7ft
Diameter	1.64ft
Span of widest fins	8.2ft
Performance	
Booster rocket thrust	10,000lb
Sustainer rocket thrust	6,835lb
Warhead	V-88 429lb fragmentation
Range	18 miles (maximum), six miles (minimum)
Maximum effective altitude	85,000ft
Speed	1,340mph
Support Equipment	
Launcher	SM-63-1 with PR-11A/AM towed transporter/ trans-loader and ZiL-157 tractor
Radar sets	P-15 "Flat Face" C-band target acquisition radar (range 155 miles) Almaz SNR-75 (RSNA-75) "Fan Song" B/E-band target tracking radar (range 75 miles) NITEL P-12/P-18 "Spoon Rest" A-band early-warning radar (range 100-150 miles). P-12NP version had a 12-element Yagi antenna on a separate ZiL vehicle from the control cabin vehicle P-10 "Knife Rest" B/C-band early-warning radar (range 173 miles). PRV-11 Vershina "Side Net" E-band height-finding radar (range 112 miles) RV electricity supply van with diesel generators

Mobility was a key to the success of the SA-2 system. A convoy of six PR-11A trans-loaders and support vehicles (like this 61st Missile Battalion procession) could be on the road within four hours of action and re-establish at an unexpected location. "Light battalions" with only one or two launchers with a "Fan Song" could also be deployed quickly to ambush positions. (via Dr. István Toperczer)

THE STRATEGIC SITUATION

M117 750lb bombs cascade from B-52F 57-0162 during an *Arc Light* mission. Aircraft that participated in the first deployment of 2nd and 320th BW B-52Fs to Andersen AFB in February 1965 had MER-6 external bomb-racks fitted. A second program, *Sun Bath*, completed wing-rack modification for 82 B-52Fs, leading to Project *Big Belly* for B-52Ds using Boeing-supplied kits, installed at maintenance centers in Oklahoma City and San Antonio. This enabled B-52Ds to carry mines, GBU-15 glide bombs, BLU-3B/-26B cluster bombs, or leaflet dispensers. Ironically, this very photograph was used on 1991 Operation *Desert Storm* propaganda leaflets warning Iraqi troops that they could face the same fate as had befallen the Viet Cong 26 years earlier. (USAF)

In August 1964 the 320th BW became the first B-52 wing to train for dual nuclear and conventional "iron bomb" delivery in advance of Vietnam involvement. Stratofortresses were intended to play a major role in the Vietnam War from the outset, with plans to use two B-52F wings (the 2nd BW from Barksdale AFB, Louisiana, and the 320th BW at Mather AFB, California) from Andersen AFB, on *Arc Light* missions in South Vietnam and Laos from February 1965. For Gen William Westmoreland, commanding US ground operations in Vietnam, the B-52 became a "priceless asset" and morale-booster for ground troops, as well as the ultimate symbol of US aerial power.

The B-52's all-weather, day or night bombing capability was unique for the USAF in Southeast Asia until the F-111A arrived in 1968. Although critics saw this use of strategic weapons as overkill, most jungle targets were inaccessible to tactical aircraft with their small bomb-loads. Experiencing an *Arc Light* attack was described by a Viet Cong official as like "being caught in an apocalypse."

In 1964 Gen Curtis LeMay, advocate of all-out commitment in a war, supported a ten-day bombing campaign against 94 North Vietnamese targets to end the war "real quick." B-52s would have mined Haiphong harbor and then area-bombed from Haiphong gradually towards Hanoi. The opening *Arc Light* offensive – SAC's first combat mission – would have involved 30 B-52Fs

For Vietnam operations B-52Fs had their white, anti-flash undersides over-painted black for night missions, while the 150 available B-52Ds had full TO-1-1-4 camouflage, as seen here on B-52D 56-0684. Its serial includes the "O for obsolete" prefix introduced in 1955 to indicate aircraft over ten years old. It is hard to imagine a suitable, equivalent prefix for B-52s in frontline service in 2018. (USAF)

bombing Phuc Yen MiG airfield in early February 1965. That mission was indefinitely postponed. President Lyndon B. Johnson decided such massive destruction was politically unacceptable and opposed LeMay's conviction that striking North Vietnam's industrial base, instead of "pecking around the edges," would force Hanoi to negotiate quickly. *Arc Light* eventually began on June 18, 1965, using streams of eight single aircraft, often against targets of dubious value.

It was understood that SAMs were being integrated into North Vietnam's Soviet-style air defense network (commanded by Col-Gen Phung The Tai) of AAA and MiGs, and that both China and the USSR were supplying equipment and training. Although no serious opposition was then expected, the Pentagon was reluctant to reveal the B-52's ECM capability. This in turn meant that missile-defended targets were avoided to prevent possible Soviet acquisition of secret equipment aboard the $8m bombers. When the North Vietnamese began to site SAMs around often-hit targets on the Laotian border in October 1966 B-52s were again kept away. Despite their powerful on-board ECM equipment, they were large targets, although F-105F *Wild Weasels* were effective in suppressing SAMs with anti-radiation missiles (see *Osprey Duel 35 F-105 Wild Weasel vs SA-2 "GUIDELINE" SAM* for further details).

THE BASES

Andersen AFB's algae-coated runway 06/24 rose 70ft along its 11,000ft, with a pronounced dip in the middle. ECM technician Peter Kuehl remembered a 0230hrs mission:

> That was quite a thrill riding a max weight B-52 in a night take-off in a heavy rainstorm. The north end of the runway went off Pati Point, which was a 500ft drop to the ocean, kind of like a big aircraft carrier.

That drop could help some ponderous B-52s as they struggled to reach the 180 knots "flaps up" speed.

To ease the pressure on Andersen 15 B-52Ds were deployed to the "Young Tiger" KC-135A base at U-Tapao RTNAB, Thailand, from April 10, 1967. After November 29 they could overfly Laos as SAC argued that, "when targets are located in the vicinity of the Demilitarized Zone [DMZ] within possible SAM lethal radius, some Laos overflight time is required for SAM evasive maneuvers."

Lt Col(then Capt) Jim Tramel's first combat mission, deployed from Barksdale AFB as an EWO in B-52D/Gs, "was in the Cambodian border region of South Vietnam so my combat experience was limited to checking my equipment and determining what radars were operating in that area. After that, we were assigned targets that were varied and in multiple areas of the Vietnam air region."

U-Tapao was only 450 miles from North Vietnamese targets, whereas Guam was 2,600 miles away. Mission times over this shorter distance were around three hours, rather than 12–14 hours from Guam or seven hours from Kadena, and B-52Ds could carry their full 64,000lb bomb-load rather than the 16 tons possible from Guam without in-flight refueling. U-Tapao's 15 B-52s were soon flying 450 of the 800 monthly *Arc Light* sorties. Tail-winds at high altitude could cut more than an hour off the Guam return flight, but crews had to breathe 100 percent oxygen when above 37,000ft, as EWO Col John Frisby remembered:

> It was a necessary safety precaution but very uncomfortable for the four- to six-hour journey to Guam. Breathing 100 percent oxygen was also a pain as it dried out the throat and forced oxygen bubbles into the inner ear so that your ears would continue to pop for hours after a flight, making it hard to get a good night's sleep.

Eleven rotational B-52D wings were involved in the war, with the nuclear deterrent being maintained by other variants. Devastating attacks on Viet Cong troops at Ia Drang in October 1965 were followed by similar missions in Operations *Cedar Falls* and *Niagara* from January 14 to March 31, 1968, when B-52Ds bombed accurately within 3,000ft of friendly troops at the beleaguered US Marine Corps Khe Sanh Combat Base. Gen Westmoreland judged that "the thing that broke their [Viet Cong's] back basically was the fire of the B-52s." They were at risk from SA-2s during many of these attacks as they were bombing from 24,000ft for greater accuracy, within slant range of missiles located in the DMZ.

ABOVE LEFT
Maintenance at Andersen AFB was undertaken by the 5,000 personnel of the 303rd Consolidated Aircraft Maintenance Wing (Provisional). The base's lack of recreation facilities led occupants to call themselves "Prisoners of Guam," or "POGs" for short. Overcrowding led to some interesting incidents, as Capt Robert Newton remembered. "I was preparing a launch and there was a truck parked in front of me. The occupant was talking to the crew chief. Along came a B-52D and hit the truck with its wingtip, throwing it 50ft with the man still in it. He didn't get hurt because he was belted in, but it destroyed the truck. The wing of the B-52D had a deep gouge in its leading edge." (USAF)

ABOVE RIGHT
Bombs were delivered in vast quantities to the aircraft by Munitions Maintenance Squadron personnel. A 27-ton load was dropped in a calculated sequence using the bomb-release interval controls – one for internal bombs and a second for pylon racks – operated by the R/N together with his D-2 "pickle switch." Bomb impacts could be observed through the B-52D's optical bombsight, located between the B/N's knees. (USAF)

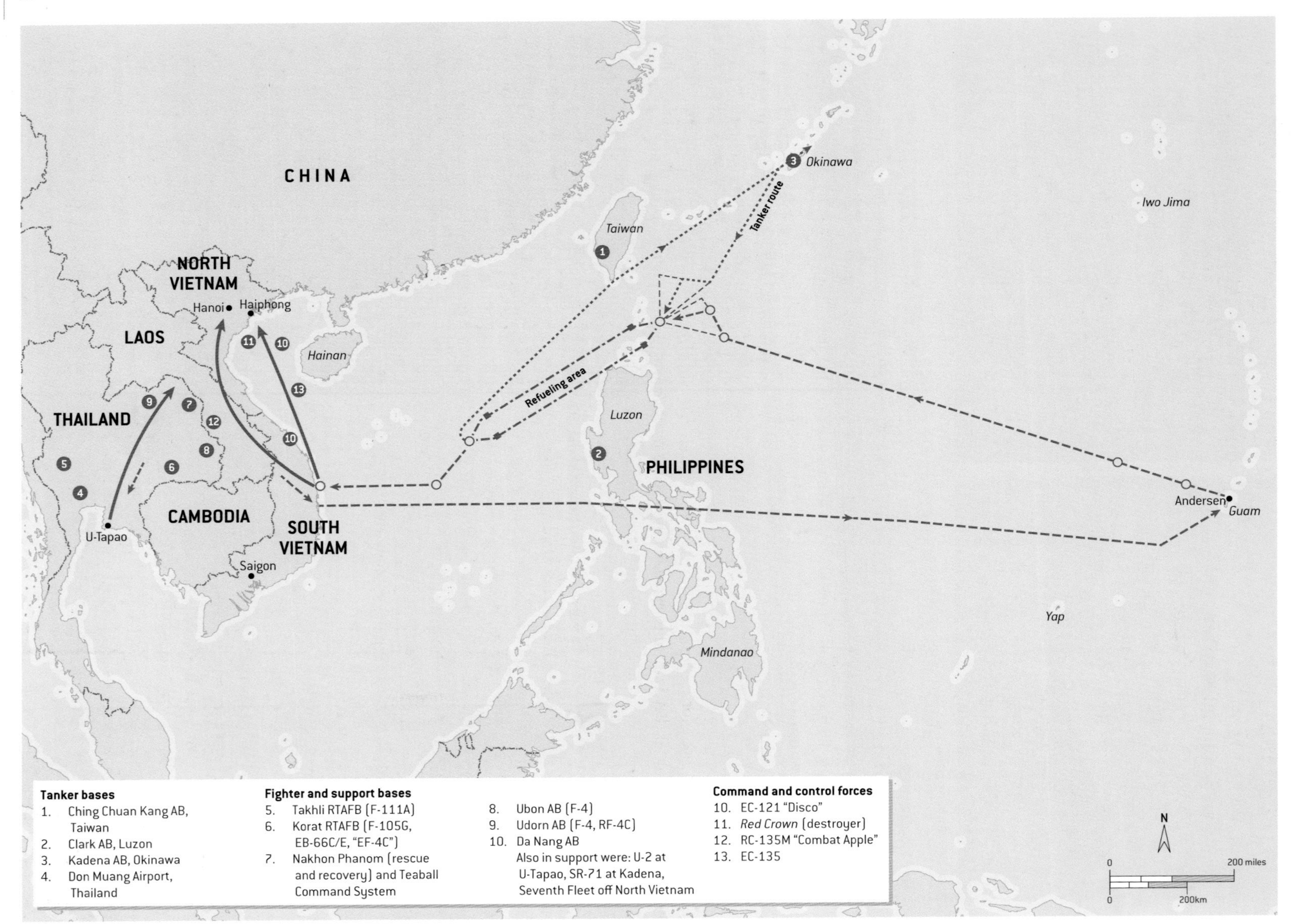

Tanker bases
1. Ching Chuan Kang AB, Taiwan
2. Clark AB, Luzon
3. Kadena AB, Okinawa
4. Don Muang Airport, Thailand

Fighter and support bases
5. Takhli RTAFB (F-111A)
6. Korat RTAFB (F-105G, EB-66C/E, "EF-4C")
7. Nakhon Phanom (rescue and recovery) and Teaball Command System
8. Ubon AB (F-4)
9. Udorn AB (F-4, RF-4C)
10. Da Nang AB

Also in support were: U-2 at U-Tapao, SR-71 at Kadena, Seventh Fleet off North Vietnam

Command and control forces
10. EC-121 "Disco"
11. *Red Crown* (destroyer)
12. RC-135M "Combat Apple"
13. EC-135

THE DEFENDERS

A preserved North Vietnamese SA-2 from the 257th Missile Regiment, poised on its SM-63-1 launcher. This unit was tasked with the defense of Kep air base and the Lang Son to Hanoi road during *Linebacker II*. To the right is a ZiL-157 truck with a P-15 "Flat Face" early-warning radar mounted on it. Although the SA-2 was fast and deadly, accounting for 205 US aircraft, including 72 in 1972, its guidance system relied on vacuum tube technology and primitive computing devices, requiring great skill on the part of its "Fan Song" launch crew when they were assigned targets by their headquarters staff. (via Dr. István Toperczer)

Although almost obsolescent in Soviet use by the late 1960s, SA-2 "Guideline" (SA-75M *Dvina* or V-750M) missiles directly threatened US aircraft in Vietnam after the shoot-down of a USAF F-4C Phantom II on July 24, 1965 by a 236th SAM Regiment missile. Four sites had initially been detected near Hanoi following the introduction of SA-2s by Soviet PVO-Strany missile regiments in April 1965, and this number had dramatically risen to 63 sites by December. Anti-SAM *Iron Hand* attacks had commenced three days after the F-4 shoot-down, but these did little to prevent the establishment of additional sites – there were more than 150 by December 1966.

Some 200 missiles were launched in 1965, downing 13 US aircraft. Although there was considerable data available from Cuban experience and CIA-obtained documents on the SA-2's capability, the US government's response was initially cautious. The Joint Chiefs of Staff (JCS), on the other hand, wanted the new sites destroyed as fast as they appeared.

B-52s faced little opposition during *Arc Light* missions unless they ventured near the DMZ or into southern North Vietnam. EWOs knew that SAM operators could only briefly use "Fan Song" if they wanted to avoid being attacked by *Wild Weasels*, and their

SA-2 sites were protected by AAA batteries, and extra guns were sometimes set up around empty sites, with dummy missiles made from bamboo and rice straw to lure tactical strike aircraft into "flak traps." The distinctive "flower" pattern of access roads on the site was usually camouflaged with nets, foliage, newly planted trees, and fast-growing bamboo. (USAF)

OPPOSITE

Bases and routes for B-52s and support aircraft during *Linebacker II*.

This 1965 photograph shows how SA-2 sites were set out on cultivated land to aid camouflage. Six missile launchers were arranged around one or two "Fan Song" vans and their support vehicles. The missiles' status was monitored by a technical officer in the "Fan Song" van. (USAF)

radar searches were usually followed by a salvo of SA-2s fuzed to detonate at a pre-determined altitude. If the *Weasels* reported a SAM threat B-52s immediately diverted to secondary targets, abandoning a third of all their primary missions. Peter Kuehl recalled:

> EWOs and tail-gunners were real jumpy on their first trip North. Until the B-52s started going North in later missions, the EWOs didn't have a whole lot to do, although they had to be ready all the time. Training missions that I rode along on in the States always had several runs against ECM sites scattered all over the USA. With the primitive receivers they had at the time I don't know how they handled these runs without having prior knowledge of the frequencies to expect. At the time [until 1964] the B-52s were equipped with the AIL/Collins AN/APR-9 receiver of near-World War II vintage for high-band emissions and the Raytheon AN/APR-14 panoramic radar receiver for lower bands. I remember the AN/APR-14 was handy on the flightline because we could tune into TV audio and listen to programs while working in the EWO's position.

The first SA-2 launch against a B-52F occurred in September 1966 over the DMZ. A 454th BW EWO detected "Fan Song" emissions and engaged deceptive jamming while the pilot abandoned the bomb-run and headed out to sea. Two SA-2s from a ZiL-157 mobile launcher exploded some 3,000ft above the Stratofortress.

Although B-52s avoided North Vietnam, Hanoi was preparing for heavier attacks closer to home. In January 1969 personnel from the 238th, 258th, 274th, and 236th Missile Regiments, together with pilots from several fighter squadrons, held seminars to discuss how to blunt the threat posed by the American bomber. A manual on SAM techniques and an air-defense plan for Hanoi and Haiphong were produced following the meetings. In September 1971 the Vietnamese Peoples' Air Force (VPAF) calculated that the US was about to launch the "imperialists' second war of destruction." It deduced that B-52s had 16 active electronic jammers, two anti-radar chaff dispensers, and Quail decoy missiles.

The SA-2 was North Vietnam's principal response, supported by fighters and AAA. A network of radar stations, each with up to nine different radar types, had been established, together with 1,350 AAA weapons including eight 100mm batteries in Hanoi. Guns, however, were only effective up to 6,000ft below the B-52s' usual altitude.

LINEBACKER APPROACHES

From February 1972 the bombers flew record sortie rates, extending into North Vietnam with raids on fuel stores and railway yards near Vinh and Bai Thuong airfield that involved brief penetrations with minimum SAM risk. When Gen Vo Nguyen Giap launched a full-scale invasion of South Vietnam on March 30, 1972, supported by mobile AAA and SAM units, it prompted a major US aerial response that included extra B-52s as most US ground troops had been withdrawn. Reorganized under five-stage *Bullet Shot* deployments, the B-52 force was enlarged (and the loss of

OPPOSITE
VNA SAM battalion locations (typical), MiG-capable airfields, support aircraft locations, and B-52 routes for December 18–21, 1972 *Linebacker II* missions.

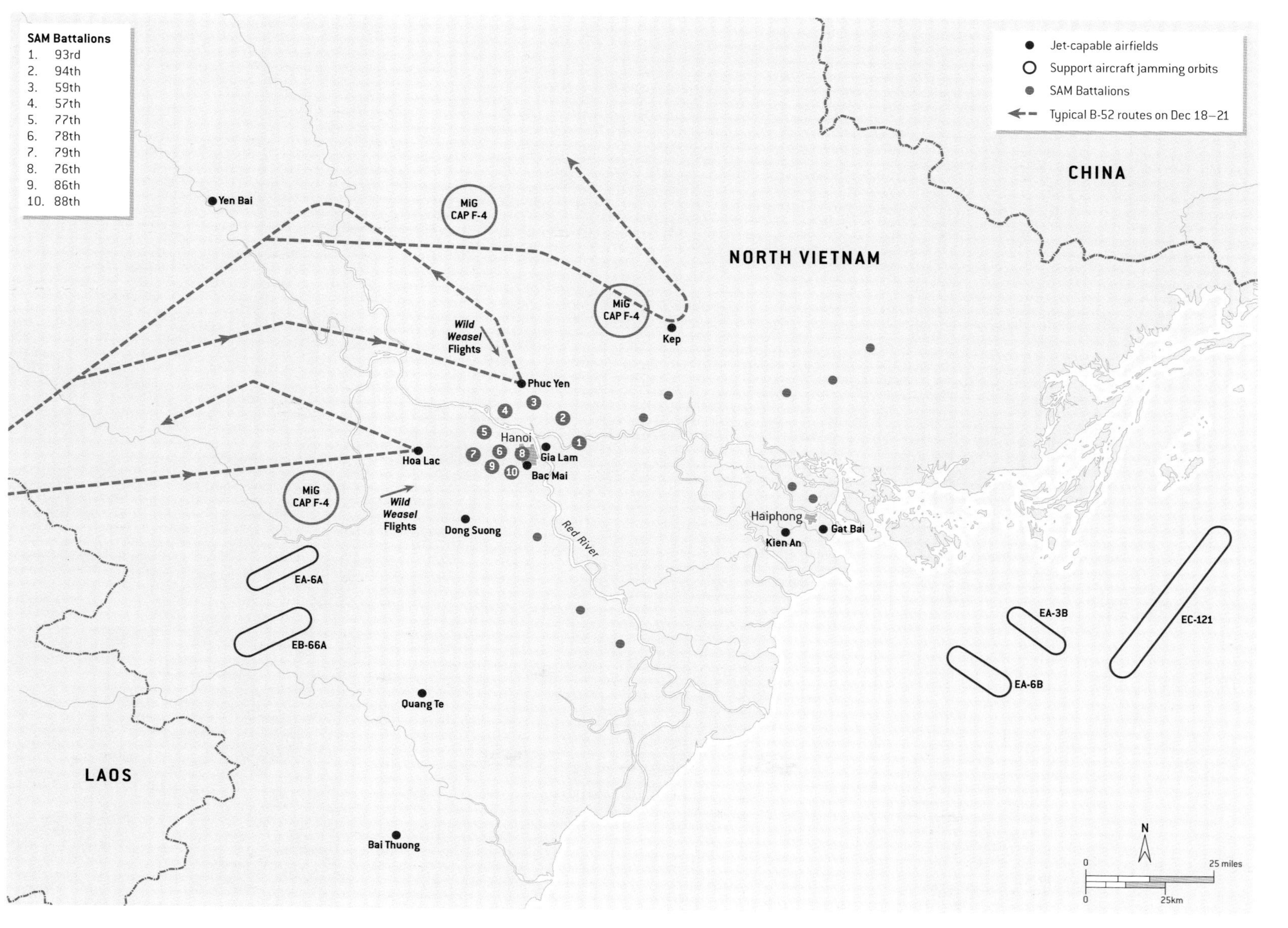

SAM Battalions
1. 93rd
2. 94th
3. 59th
4. 57th
5. 77th
6. 78th
7. 79th
8. 76th
9. 86th
10. 88th
Jet-capable airfields
Support aircraft jamming orbits
SAM Battalions
Typical B-52 routes on Dec 18–21
CHINA
NORTH VIETNAM
LAOS
Yen Bai
MiG CAP F-4
MiG CAP F-4
Kep
Wild Weasel Flights
Phuc Yen
Hanoi
Gia Lam
Bac Mai
Hoa Lac
MiG CAP F-4
Wild Weasel Flights
Dong Suong
Red River
Haiphong
Gat Bai
Kien An
EA-6A
EB-66A
EA-3B
EA-6B
EC-121
Quang Te
Bai Thuong
N
0 25 miles
0 25km

D-models compensated) through the arrival of 57 B-52Ds and no fewer than 145 52Gs, flown to Andersen for the 72nd SW(P) – a total that comprised almost half of SAC's heavy bomber force for Operation *Linebacker*.

Shifting from support of South Vietnamese Army (ARVN) ground troops, the "bombing line" moved progressively closer to Hanoi throughout April 1972. Strikes on the 16th of that month as part of Operation *Freedom Porch Bravo* prefigured the *Linebacker II* attacks of December 1972 in using tactical aircraft (in this case US Navy A-6A Intruders) to attack SAM sites near Haiphong and USAF F-4 Phantom IIs to lay radar-deflecting chaff corridors to mask the B-52s. Thirty-five SA-2s were reported, although they appeared to be unguided or negated by US ECM, increasing faith in B-52 self-protection measures.

The first 30-aircraft B-52 *Linebacker I* attacks on southern North Vietnam on June 8 constituted a major air assault and reinvigorated South Vietnamese resistance, forcing Giap to abandon his ill-advised Spring Offensive. *Linebacker I* ended on October 22 with hopes of peace negotiations.

After 112,000 missions without loss, several B-52s were damaged during the Spring Offensive, including Capt Ken Curry's D-model which had a drop tank punctured by a "track on jam" SA-2 launch during an April 9 Vinh attack. Two more were damaged in November 1972 and shooting down a B-52 became a major propaganda aim for the North Vietnamese. Great emphasis was placed upon capturing B-52 crew members and Radio Hanoi regularly announced Stratofortress "shoot-downs" throughout 1971. SAM sites were established near Tchepone, in Laos, and they remained undetected by US reconnaissance aircraft until they fired at B-52s.

The loss of B-52D "Olive 02" in November 1972 was a considerable propaganda boost for SA-2 crews, whose enthusiasm appears to be choreographed by their senior officer (bottom right). Foliage was often used to camouflage the missiles. (via Dr. István Toperczer)

MiG-21 pilots also trained hard for a B-52 kill, and Vu Dinh Rang was the first to claim damage to one over Laos on November 20, 1971. Another attempt by Dinh Ton in October of that same year, flying from a forward airfield, was frustrated by radar jamming. Other pilots also struggled with the latter, being unable to locate the bombers or penetrate the chaff. SA-2 operators came close to success in April 1972 when Capt John Alward's B-52D 56-0665 was hit, knocking out two engines, causing severe fuel leaks, and punching 400 holes in the airframe. Diverted to Da Nang in poor weather and darkness, he found the base under rocket and

Shrike-armed F-105G Thunderchiefs provided essential SAM suppression for most B-52 missions. Before *Linebacker II*, they sometimes flew risky close-escort for the bombers. F-105G 63-8359 was flying to the left of a November 16, 1972 *Arc Light* cell when two SAMs emerged through thick overcast. They were fended off by the B-52s' ECM but the second SA-2 hit the Weasel and Maj Norman Meier and Capt Ken Theate ejected. F-105F 62-4416 was the G-model test-bed in 1966, proving the concept with four others in Vietnam that year and returning in 1972 to fly with the 17th Wild Weasel Squadron/388th TFW from Korat RTAFB. The jet was nicknamed *Little Stevie* and *Vegetable*. (USAF)

mortar attack as he came in to land. Alward touched down, but his drag chute cable had been severed by shrapnel. He made a "go-around" landing, just avoiding a minefield at the end of the runway.

On November 22, 1972, an expert team working with the 263rd Missile Battalion at Nghe An finally downed a Stratofortress. U-Tapao-based "Olive 02" (B-52D 55-0110 of the 96th BW) was hit during a post-target turn (PTT) after bombing in an 18-aircraft wave near Vinh, the missile starting fires in the rear fuselage and wings. *Wild Weasel* support for the flight was led, in F-105G 63-8285, by Col Dan Barry, who recalled the communications problems with SAC aircraft:

> Unfortunately, the "Buffs" were never on our radio frequency so we never received any changes to TOTs [Time on Targets] or ingress tracks, nor were any advisory we'd transmit on SAM signals received. Although one of the 17th WWS [F-105G] crews fired a pre-emptive Shrike, I don't believe any of us received a "Fan Song" signal. I recall only one SAM being fired, and it seemed to go nearly vertically before we saw it explode at altitude. I remember finally turning towards our egress heading and seeing an explosion at altitude and flaming wreckage falling nearly 100 miles away.

The stricken B-52D struggled towards Thailand as fire gradually consumed it. Without electrical power, Capt Norbert "Oz" Ostrozny glided across the Thai border after his last engine gave out. The crew ejected at 15,000ft when a 20ft section of the right wing separated. All were rescued by a CH-53 helicopter, but the propaganda bonus for North Vietnam was considerable. It seemed likely that no "Fan Song" signals were transmitted because the operators were triangulating the target with search radars and passing this information to the "Fan Song" – a technique that would have worse consequences for the B-52 force in December. The incident also showed that chaff corridors, dropped from high altitude by F-4 Phantom IIs on either side of the B-52s' ingress route, were imperfect shields as unpredicted high winds blew the chaff away.

For the following three weeks B-52s were ordered to abort several attacks when SA-2s were detected, despite active SAM suppression by tactical aircraft. SAM operators passed the methods that achieved the November 22 success on to all other batteries, who reconstructed the event on their "Spoon Rest" and "Fan Song" radar screens and practiced interception techniques. SAC's repetitive bomber routes, speeds, and altitudes clearly assisted SAM operators, particularly those manning fixed sites around Hanoi and Haiphong where their radar coverage overlapped.

Using mobile SA-2 launchers, like those at Vinh, meant relocating them after each firing to elude *Wild Weasels*. Laborious transporting, relocating and re-calibrating the fragile SA-2 equipment blunted its effectiveness, but the advantages of being able to ambush US aircraft in southern North Vietnam were considerable. Firing randomly at B-52 cells could make them divert from the target, but from late November 1972 onwards B-52s were ordered to "press on."

Using similar procedures against B-52s and EB-66 jamming aircraft, "Fan Song" operators could detect aircraft passively with "track on jam" by targeting the source of the aircraft's jamming without using the radar's fire-control system, and thereby revealing their position. "Fan Song" crews used B-52 jamming emissions to locate the target in azimuth and transmit that information to the missile. If the calculations were correct, the SA-2's proximity fuze would detonate near a "straight-and-level" target at the correct moment without precise range statistics. The destruction of Ostrozny's B-52 was possibly through a "track on jam" launch in which the "Fan

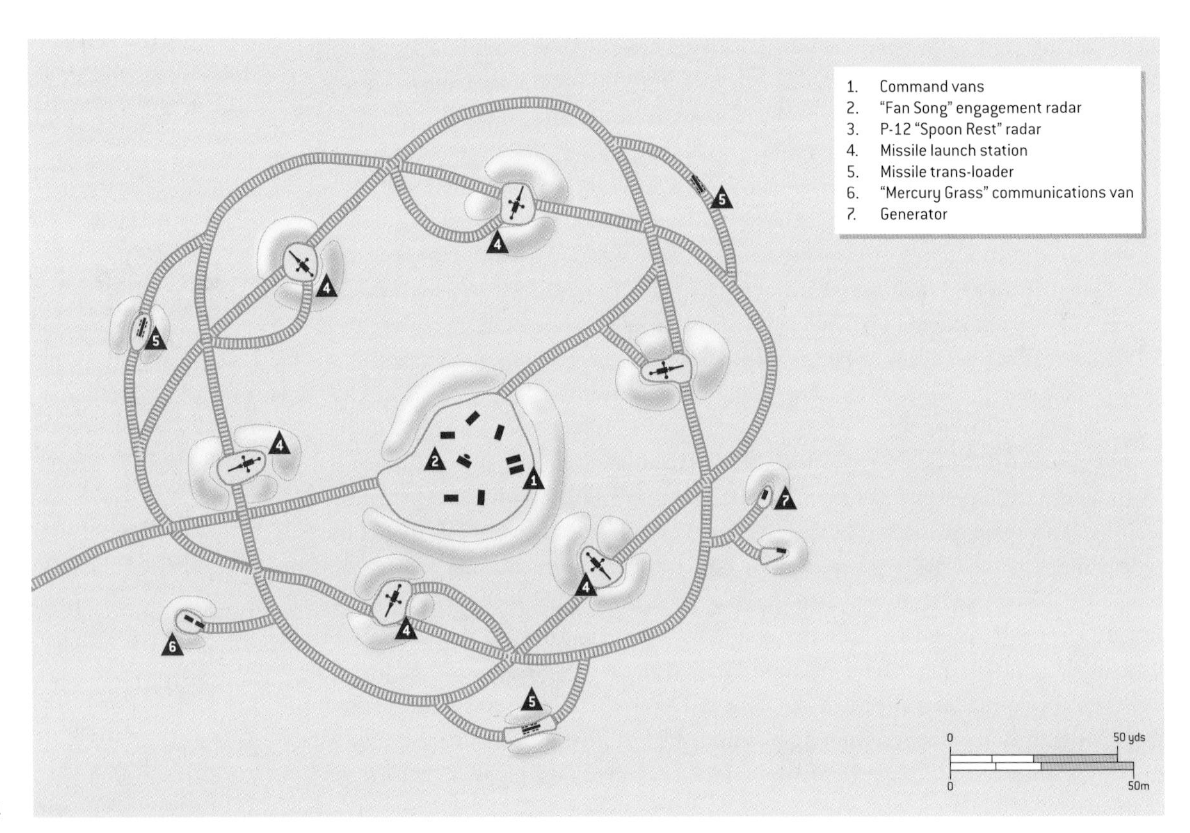

Song" was used for a few seconds in the final part of the SA-2's trajectory to provide terminal guidance.

MAXIMUM EFFORT

By October 1972 North Vietnam's continued intransigence persuaded President Richard Nixon to increase the pressure with *Linebacker II*. The original three-night plan for heavy B-52 attacks avoided the VPAF's 204 MiGs and the daytime, optically aimed SA-2s of the North Vietnamese Army (NVA). Bombing from altitudes in excess of 32,000ft put the B-52s above AAA (which failed to deter the gunners from prodigious firing), but within the SA-2's optimum envelope. SAC assumed that the B-52s' sophisticated ECM could cope with SAMs. *Wild Weasel* pioneer Capt Ed Sandelius commented that within the 1965 USAF, "SAC had about 85 percent of the electronic warfare equipment and EWOs." However, many doubted that the primary nuclear deterrent should be exposed to such risks.

As previous bombing campaigns against North Vietnam had not altered its attitudes, Nixon wanted "something new, and that means we will have to hit Hanoi and Haiphong with B-52s." Hanoi's 361st Air Defense Division SAM batteries, in three regiments, each with three SA-2 battalions (advised by Russian Col-Gen Anotoliy Khyupenen), were ordered to save their missiles for B-52 attacks rather than tactical aircraft, and increase AAA and fighter protection for their sites. Technical sub-units were established, each with two SA-2 assembly and testing teams working 24 hours a day. Dispersed field centers were also set up to prepare missiles.

In August 1972 Eighth Air Force commander, World War II fighter ace Lt Gen Gerald W. Johnson, was asked to plan decisive strikes. Extensive radar photography of the Hanoi area in August identified targets and radar offsets. Nixon's campaign, which Johnson was eventually told to execute with only 72 hours' notice,

The B-52D's planned phase-out was delayed by its vital performance in Vietnam. The aircraft's critically important ECM antenna "farm" is visible on the underside of the fuselage of B-52D 56-0671. The jammer suite was so powerful that on several continental US training flights populated areas lost television and radio transmissions over hundreds of square miles when jammers were accidentally turned on. B-52Ds had no fuel dumping system, and excess fuel had to be burned off to achieve landing weight. Later models could dump fuel, but remaining wing-tank fuel had to be equally balanced before landing to keep the flexible wings level while taxiing. (USAF)

was to be "a three-day maximum effort, repeat maximum effort of B-52/ Tacair strikes."

However, the detailed instructions that SAC commander Gen John C. Meyer (also a World War II fighter ace) and his staff issued in December differed substantially from Johnson's plan. Involving only JCS target recommendations and support from Seventh Air Force tactical aircraft, they were issued directly by SAC to the wartime B-52 bases. Stratofortresses were to operate within traditional, rigid SAC tactics that were unsuited to the situation over North Vietnam, and these would cost the bomber force dearly. Crucially, *Linebacker II* did not begin with a "maximum effort" to destroy the enemy's SAM sites because it was assumed that MiGs would be a greater threat, and there were more urgent logistical and infrastructure targets for what was assumed to be only a three-night effort.

Visibility from the cockpit of a B-52 was limited, but adequate, and the most common view for pilots was of other cell members as they worked at keeping the correct spacing between bombers. The upward-firing ejection seat fitted in the aircraft was allegedly designed for short pilots with long arms. The only place crew members could stand upright in the cabin was on the ladder to the lower deck. EWOs, in the dark rear cabin, sometimes felt that they only became important during the combat phase of a mission, which could last just 20 minutes in a 16-hour flight. (USAF)

THE COMBATANTS

B-52 CREW

A B-52D/G crew comprised five officers and an enlisted gunner, with occasional instructors or observers. The pilot (aircraft commander) needed physical strength to maneuver the big bomber and particular skill for in-flight refueling – often considered the most demanding in-flight task. Managing a B-52D, without powered controls, was often compared with driving an 18-wheel truck without power steering, brakes, or automatic transmission during the rush hour. His co-pilot was principally concerned with fuel and engine management.

Fifteen feet behind them, in a rearward-facing, windowless "defense team" position, was the Electronic Countermeasures Officer (later known as the Electronic Warfare Officer, EWO, EW, "Ewee," or "E-Dub"). Many EWOs were re-trained navigators and during the *Chrome Dome* airborne alert era some were instructed in fuel, electrical, and hydraulics system management so that they could take over during a pilot's sleep break. "E-Dub" (as the crew "secretary") took aboard the large metal "secrets box" with classified documents and red-covered books on defenses, targets, call-signs, and codes. EWOs' knowledge made them particularly valuable PoWs, and many were subjected to inhumane treatment while in captivity.

An EWO was also the HF radio operator, handling communications with the command post, but in high-threat environments he was principally the aircraft's main protector. Pre-flight, EWOs checked the ECM antennas and transmitters, aluminized mylar chaff and flare dispensers in the dark, and 30ft-long "47 section" ahead of the B-52D tail gunner's compartment. In flight, they sometimes had to crawl along the

The crew of B-52G 58-0230 line up before another *Linebacker II* mission from Guam. Crews were given a number (e.g. E-12, signifying an experienced crew) and their work and social lives were carefully monitored to pre-empt any potential safety risks. The B-52G was designed in 1956 to compensate for problems with the Convair B-58A Hustler that could have left SAC short of bombers. (via Terry Panopalis)

cold, dark cat-walk on a 100ft journey aft to check on the gunner if his intercom failed. EWOs also took celestial observations for the navigators through a periscope sextant, extended from the upper fuselage, which gave a good view of the aircraft's upper surfaces in an emergency.

Essentially, the EWO's task was to conduct a duel between enemy radars and his ECM, employing radar jamming and chaff dispensing and providing the pilot with instructions on how best to perform effective evasive maneuvers to break radar lock or defeat an inbound SAM. Although EWOs were briefed on the location of known SAM sites and associated early-warning radar, their ingenuity and initiative were essential during *Linebacker II*. As Vietnamese ground radars were more powerful than the aircraft's jamming capacity, at close range they had to use their equipment skillfully, directing and modulating its energy towards imminent threats.

For *Linebacker*, EWOs tested their jammers briefly before entering the threat area, alerting ground radars within 125 miles to the B-52s' approach, distance, and arrival time. Testing also tended to disguise enemy radars, so some EWOs briefly turned off the equipment nearer the target, revealing many additional emitters. Soviet analysts found B-52 jamming to be most effective at a range of around 15 miles and an altitude of 32,000ft.

Using similar equipment in both the B-52D and B-52G, the "E-Dub" worked mainly with the rectangular screen of his AN/ALR-20 panoramic receiver set – a big orange TV screen when switched off – monitoring, assessing, and prioritizing numerous electronic emissions between 20 MHz and 20 GHz. The latter were presented as seven "stacked" horizontal traces, the "E-Dub" scanning them with a manual "dot" and marking signal positions with a grease pencil. With his head in the "scope," he operated the switches by touch, like the navigator. His AN/APR-25 radar homing and warning receiver showed strobes extending over concentric rings, indicating the range and strength of hostile signals. A "one ring" call told the crew a SAM uplink had been acquired and "two rings" indicated that a missile had been launched. When Capt Silverio Barroqueiro, EWO in B-52G 57-6481 "Brass 02" on Night Three of *Linebacker II*, saw 3.5 rings on his scope he knew an SA-2's uplink guidance signal had locked onto his aircraft, and it was hit seconds later.

If a targeted aircraft maneuvered to break a "Fan Song" lock-on, the SAM site would then take about a minute to re-acquire the target. Its signal changed in frequency once the missile entered firing mode, requiring more intense jamming against the uplink signal. "Corkscrew" turning maneuvers or dives to avoid SA-2s separated a cell, and aircraft risked collision as they attempted to re-join.

At the optimum range EWOs tuned their jammers to disrupt hostile radar signals, changing the fan-shaped jamming frequency whenever the enemy operator moved to a different wavelength. B-52 jamming emissions were projected below the fuselage, with patterns also around the nose and tail. As *Linebacker* EW Capt Ken Nocito pointed out, the jammers "required constant tuning and monitoring." At one point he had 50 different hostile radar signals on his scope, all requiring attention. Selecting the right control to match the changes quickly, or out-guessing the "Fan Song" operators, was a matter of experience, with an element of luck. Multiple, manually aimed SA-2s that relied on altitude information provided by dispersed radar sites or MiGs could overwhelm the B-52's defensive measures.

Concentrated jamming by a triangular cell formation with aircraft at a 45 degrees back-angle from the leader at 500ft below the others was most effective. EWOs used two General Electric AN/ALT-22 or AN/ALT-6B continuous-wave transmitters, two AN/ALT-28s against "Fan Song," and two AN/ALT-28s against the SA-2 uplink. As Col J. E. Frisby explained, "the AN/ALT-28 used a programmable pulse jamming mode specifically intended to defeat the "Fan Song" track-while-scan radar, while the AN/ALT-22 and -6B used a programmable sweep jamming mode." AN/ALT-22s and AN/ALT-28s were also used against height-finding radars and a Northrop AN/ALT-32 jammed communications.

B-52D EWO Col John E. Frisby flew combat missions from Andersen AFB and U-Tapao RTNAB. (Col John E. Frisby)

EWO'S VIEW

The following extract is from *Stuck in Las Vegas* (unpublished), written by former B-52D EWO Col J. E. Frisby. He flew numerous combat missions from Andersen AFB and U-Tapao RTNAB:

> The EW could detect SAM radar in one of two ways, or both simultaneously. First, just like the strobe from the search or acquisition radars, the SAM radar would present two

B-52D COCKPIT

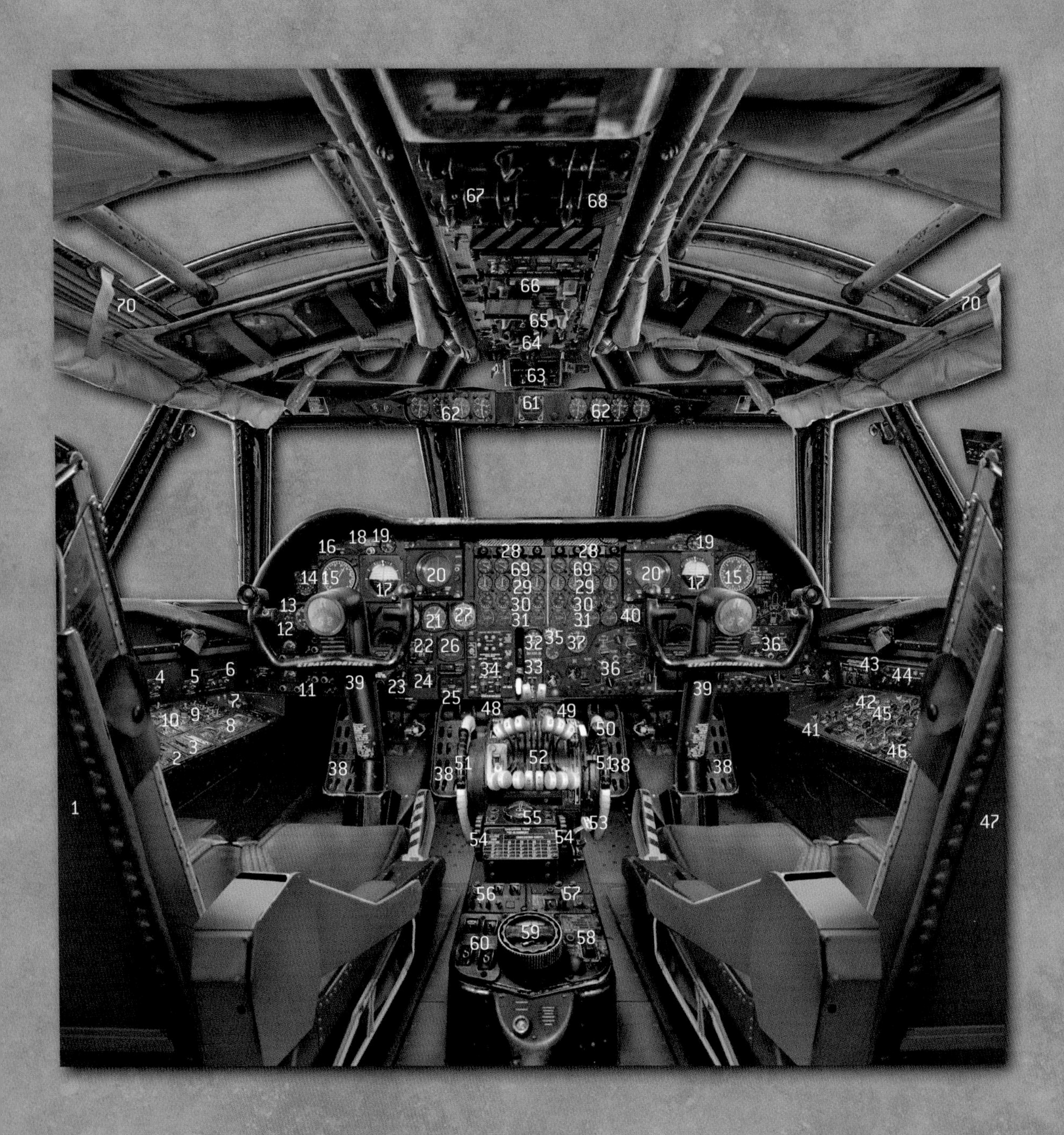

1. Pilot's seat
2. Wing flap emergency switches
3. Anti-icing control panel
4. Autopilot servo panel
5. Special Weapons Emergency Separation panel
6. Navigation lights controls
7. AN/APS-54 radar warning receiver indicator
8. Oxygen converter quantity gauges
9. Liaison radio control panel
10. Pilot's interphone panel
11. T-18 control panel
12. Bomb-bay door switch
13. Mach meter
14. Clock
15. Directional indicator
16. "Bombs released" light
17. Attitude indicator
18. Hydraulic pack pressure "low" master light
19. Clearance plane indicator
20. Terrain display indicator
21. Vertical speed indicator
22. Autopilot turn control selector switch
23. Engine fire detection switch
24. Navigation system select switch panel
25. Anti-icing controls
26. Distance counter
27. Flight command indicator
28. Engine fire warning lights
29. Tachometers
30. Exhaust gas temperature gauges
31. Fuel flow meters
32. Wing flap position indicator
33. Anti-skid switch
34. Landing gear controls
35. Tail compartment pressure indicator
36. Fuel system controls
37. Total fuel flow indicator
38. Rudder pedals
39. Pilot's and co-pilot's control yokes
40. Radar altimeter
41. Interphone power switch panel
42. Air bleed manifold pressure gauges
43. Air bleed manifold interconnect switches
44. Engine ignition and starter switches
45. Refueling panel
46. AGM-28 Hound Dog emergency control panel
47. Co-pilot's seat
48. Parking brake lever
49. Crosswind crab undercarriage position indicator
50. Drag 'chute lever
51. Stabilizer trim wheel and indicators
52. Throttle levers
53. Wing flap lever
54. Autopilot turn and pitch controller
55. Turn knob
56. Autopilot switch panel
57. Navigation system select panel
58. Emergency alarm switch and monitor light
59. Rudder trim and crosswind control centering control
60. Yaw damping control switches
61. Magnetic standby compass
62. Oil pressure gauges
63. Air refueling panel
64. UHF command radio control
65. Omni range radio control
66. Standby UHF command radio control panel
67. Overhead lighting panel
68. Jettison control panel
69. Engine pressure ratio gauges
70. Overhead sun hoods

strobes side by side on his receiver traces – a tell-tale sign that a higher frequency radar had been detected. Those strobes pulsated rapidly and, like the search radar signal, grew in height and strength as the distance between their location and the approaching target closed. One strobe was attempting to track and refine target elevation while the other tracked and refined on-target azimuth. The twin strobes looked like a pair of snake's teeth, and they corresponded to the deadly sound given off when the EWO "went manual" and listened to them. They sounded exactly like a rattlesnake about to strike.

The second method of detection was with the AN/APR-25 warning receiver. This was a neat little device mounted above or next to the AN/ALR-20 receiver and had a small round screen with range rings that resembled a radar scope. It also had two rows of illuminating square buttons beneath the scope, each with a type of corresponding threat such as "AAA," "SAM" or "AI" [airborne interceptor], "launch" (missile guidance beam) etc. which would illuminate if that type of signal was detected.

The AN/APR-25 would also present a strobe that pointed in the relative direction of the threat and increased in size with an increase in signal strength. The strobes were also visually coded as a line of dots or dashes in order to distinguish the different threats. The AN/APR-25 also gave off audio signals that corresponded to the threats – the rattlesnake rattle of a SAM, the distinctive "swish, swish, swish" for AAA or a high-pitched squeal for an interceptor. Once a threat signal was detected, the EWO had to immediately notify the crew, since he was the only one who had the capability to detect the threat, recognize its specific type and characteristics and select the appropriate countermeasures systems to employ against it. There was no automation in the process.

The EWO had a variety of jamming systems to choose from. The joke among EWOs was, "You have 356 different switches, dials and gauges to choose from. So many choices, so little time." And time was the key. From the moment a threat signal was detected, the aircraft was susceptible to attack. The EWO had only fractions of a second to recognize the signal, select the appropriate types and numbers of jammers and other countermeasures such as chaff and flares, turn them on and refine the jamming signals over the threat signal. He then continued to monitor the threat signal for its reaction to the countermeasures, like changing its frequency or mode of operation and refine his countermeasure against those changes. The effect of successful employment of countermeasures would be to blank the scope of the target-tracking radar completely with noise, or generate false strobes or even multiple false targets to hide the radar return of the real aircraft and confuse the operator.

Col Frisby provided the following account of a 1969 mission from Guam:

Cocooned in the "cave" of the EWO's position, I stared at the equipment. The beeps and squeaks of incoming radar signals chirped through my headset. The green glow from the AN/ALR-20 main receiver and ANAPR-25 RWR [radar warning receiver] were the primary sources of light, with backlit lettering from over 100 dials, switches and gauges adding to the dim illumination. I could make out the low growls of the conical scans of B-52 gunners' radars as they probed the sky around the formations of bombers. Listening to the audio characteristics of a signal was better than 50 percent of the skill required of an EWO to identify it and relate its characteristics, which had been committed to memory, so that he could understand how it might affect the mission.

During the bomb-run each aircraft had its own designated target coordinates, so even though they would be in formation roughly 1,000ft apart and altitude-stacked up or down by 500ft, each aircraft would be on its own bomb-run. The trick for the pilot when maneuvering [to avoid SAMs] was to roll out of the maneuver approximately 20 seconds before bomb release with the PDI [pilot direction indicator – a steering needle on the main instrument panel tied into the bomb system. When the indicator was centered, the aircraft was aimed directly at the target] centered on the pre-planned bombing altitude. Obviously you didn't want to maneuver during the bomb-run as it greatly increased the potential for inaccuracies. On the other hand, if you really were a target, better to do whatever it took to avoid a shoot-down.

Jim Cichocki demonstrates his uncanny strength as a B-52D bomb-loader. (Author's collection)

Nearing the target, with two minutes to go, I stared more intently at the receivers. So far, so good. Almost as if it had read my mind, the dreaded snake-teeth signals of a SAM radar appeared, along with a strobe at "12 o'clock" and the tell-tale rattle from the RWR. "SAM, 12 o'clock, low PRF [pulse repetition frequency], maneuver." It looked as if we were going to have to fly directly at the missile site in order to strike the target. Almost as soon as my call was out the signals jumped in height on the receiver, the RWR indications changed to a rapid blinking strobe and the "high PRF" light illuminated.

"Ninety seconds" called the navigator. The signals continued to grow and the strobe swung from left to right as the pilot maneuvered. As I noticed each change in direction I reached down and back to my left and hit the "manual dispense" program on the chaff dispenser. That would present several large "blooms" on the SAM radar scope, each in a different location and heading, and hopefully confuse the operator. With all 15 aircraft dispensing chaff, maneuvering and jamming, we hoped we could hide in the noise created on the SAM operator's scope. The only problem was that all 15 aircraft were heading towards the same point from the same direction, so a good operator might be able to analyze what was going on and find "tail-end Charlie" in all that mess.

"Sixty seconds." The signal was still there. I could hear it when listening through the jamming in manual mode. I was doing everything I knew to counter the SAM threat. It was only one signal, so I had piled all eight transmitters available in that band on top of it and set four to one mode of pulse jamming and another to sweep jamming. It was frustrating that I couldn't shoot something at it. "'Hammer' [F-105G] has acquired," came the call from *Iron Hand* [*Wild Weasel*]. Well, at least *they* could shoot at it.

"Thirty seconds. Doors." The Navigator made the call to open the bomb-bay doors. That was something you wanted to delay until the last possible moment, as opening the bomb-bay doors made the "Buff" a bigger radar target reflector than it already was, and much easier for a threat radar to acquire. "Come on. Come on!" I thought, then I called "Launch!" as the launch light on the RWR illuminated and a large strobe appeared on the receiver at the frequency of a missile guidance beam. The SAM had caught the B-52s at the worst possible moment. If they stopped maneuvering to release weapons they were sitting ducks. If they didn't, it would mean withholding the weapons – and they were still sitting ducks.

"Twenty seconds. Stop maneuver. Level" called the pilot. "I have visual on the missile at '12 o'clock'" called the co-pilot. [On a count of ten] the aircraft lurched as it started to shed 60,000lb. "5, 10, 15, 20, release complete, doors closed, maneuver" called the navigator. The aircraft lurched again as the pilot yanked it into a maximum bank away from the missile. "Second missile, 'one o'clock'" called the co-pilot. The signal went down and all indications from the RWR stopped. "Missiles appear unguided," called the co-pilot. "They're veering away to 'three o'clock'. *Iron Hand* must have nailed it."

Photographs from a subsequent reconnaissance mission showed that the SAM site had been destroyed by bombs from the leading "Scarlet" cell of B-52s.

In many B-52 crews "E-Dub" was regarded as the "smartest guy in the jet," although his status in the crew hierarchy was just above the gunner's! His tape recorder, for electronic signals, intercom exchanges and important points in the flight for later analysis, could also entertain the crew on long flights. Pilot Gene Goss recalled that his EWO, Gene Lasater, "made the seven hours back to Andersen tolerable by plugging into the intercom system and playing Country and Western music all the way home."

EWOs spent many hours studying recorded radar audio signals during a 33-week course at Keesler AFB, Mississippi. They learned to recognize radar audio signatures, including the low-frequency pulses of long-distance search radars, the high-pitched warble of search-and-track missile-controlling radars and the rapid pulses of AAA radar or fighters' airborne signals. Col Frisby reckoned:

The process was very much like a language lab. The graduation exam consisted of listening to and correctly identifying 50 different signals. A passing grade was 100 percent.

Lt Col Jim Tramel, who completed 180.5 missions during four Southeast Asia tours for *Arc Light* and *Linebacker II*, recalled that:

> EW training was very good. The initial training was very intense and covered the various types of radars and signal intercepts that we might encounter. On almost every flight, when we were not overseas, we flew against ground simulators that emulated the different radars, including different types of threat radars. I became an EW instructor early in my career, and each simulator flight that I instructed contained SAM threats and various types of aircraft threats. Since the B-52 was not allowed over North Vietnam at the time, most EWs had no actual experience [of SAMs] and relied on simulator training. A few EWs did fly some rather special missions "up north" and did gain some [SAM] experience.

"CREW DOGS"

The navigator and radar-navigator (R/N, formerly "bombardier," but still the "crew dog" who dropped the bombs) worked in a cramped, noisy compartment with dim red lighting in the "basement," connected to the upper deck by a ladder. Nearing the target, the pilot used his PDI to steer the aircraft to the release point and the R/N placed his radar cross-hairs on the target. About a minute before arriving on target, the pilot handed control of the bomber to the R/N, who flew the B-52 until the ordnance had been released – stable flight was required for about ten seconds to guarantee accurate delivery. Precise navigation and timing were also essential over the Pacific to ensure a successful rendezvous with the Kadena-based tankers.

Upper-deck crewmen had Weber upward-firing ejection seats while the two navigators' seats fired downwards – an obvious concern if the aircraft lost power before reaching "S-1" (take-off speed). The minimum downward ejection altitude was 250ft.

The B-52D's gunner, who was also the crew's only enlisted man, controlled four M3 0.50-caliber machine guns with an MD-9 fire-control system from a confined, pressurized tail compartment that was subjected to fuselage flexing. As gunner Danny Burnett recalled:

> The "Boeing Bounce" is what they called the rough ride in a "tall tail" B-52. The tail moved three feet for every foot the nose moved, and it was considered a macho sign to have had a helmet cracked on your head from the ride.

In the confined "black hole," the R/N (background), who was usually the senior man in the B-52 crew, was last to board the aircraft. Navigators generally worked without their helmets and parachutes on. Partial-pressure suits, worn here by B-52B crewmen, were only needed above 50,000ft. Returning to base, the navigator (foreground) sometimes had to crawl along a six-inch wide walkway, through two bulkhead doors to the noisy alternator deck and forward wheel-well, without a parachute, to check with his flashlight for any hung bombs in the cavernous bomb-bay. (Boeing)

Gunners were responsible for saving many B-52Ds by giving crew members visual warning of SAMs approaching from the rear. In the B-52G/H they could monitor the positions of other rearward aircraft on radar. One of the gunner's duties was the "Bonus Deal" technique in which he directed bombing by another B-52 if it had lost its own bombing radar. The radar-less bomber positioned itself a mile behind another, whose gunner used his MD-9 fire-control radar to calculate an exact distance between the two bombers, converting distance into a time difference. On a timed release signal from the leader, the trailing B-52's R/N dropped the bombs. As B-52 radar failure was not uncommon, double "Bonus Deals" for two B-52s were occasionally needed.

Much of SAC's Stratofortress activity in Southeast Asia involved the B-52D, and many crews undertook cross-training from other models, including B-52G/Hs, through two-week B-52D "D-Difference" courses run by the 93rd BW at Castle AFB, California. On six-month temporary duty (TDY) combat tours in Southeast Asia, with only 28-day "rest and ruination" breaks, crews would operate from Andersen AFB, U-Tapao RTNAB and also (briefly) Kadena AB during extended tours that could include up to five 179-day TDYs. U-Tapao was the favorite TDY location, as Andersen offered only the most basic facilities and accommodation. During *Linebacker II*, U-Tapao crews flew between five and nine night missions in a row – more than the Andersen flyers. Several B-52 crews completed 400 missions and two reached 500. All were carefully chosen to work well together for long periods in a confined B-52. In Lt Col Jim Tramel's case, "My first two tours in Southeast Asia were with different crews, while the last two were with the same crew."

Gunner Danny Burnett strapped into his ejection seat in front of the AN/ASG-15 fire-control system, seen here in the "stowed" position, in his B-52G. On long flights an EWO often had "down time" that encouraged amusing pastimes for his close neighbor, the gunner. Danny was one such prankster. "If the gunner caught his EWO dozing off you could run his ejection seat to the 'full up' position then pull the circuit breaker. This worked really well on the 'not very tall'. When the EWO woke he might find that he could not reach the microphone switch to use the intercom, much less the floor, and he would flail about until either he realized why the seat didn't move and got the gunner to reset the switch, or he would un-strap and start troubleshooting the seat." (Author's collection)

Preparation for a mission involved up to three hours of briefing and pre-flighting the aircraft. If any technical problems could not be resolved before engine start time the crew would have to pack their gear and "bag drag" to a spare aircraft, waiting with its engines running. Andersen-based B-52s were maintained by units in the "Bicycle Works." Bombs were loaded by teams working 12-hour shifts, seven days a week, loading pre-packaged racks for the bomb-bays and hanging bombs from wing racks. Missions usually lasted up to 13 uncomfortable hours, rather than three to five hours for "U-T" flights, including at least one refueling, often in turbulent air conditions. The on-board coffee hot-cups were essential for keeping crews alert.

THE SUPPORTERS

Support squadrons' jamming or "chaffing" was vital in the anti-SAM effort. Fighter pilot Lt Col Fred Sheffler was a *Linebacker* "Chaffeteer":

> One very undesirable mission that fell to the 336th TFS was dropping chaff. We flew as an eight-ship, line abreast formation. Each F-4E Phantom II had one AN/ALE-38 chaff pod or four [M-129] chaff bombs and an ECM pod in the left, forward missile well. We replaced the *Wild Weasels* in being the first jets on target.

A 50-mile-long chaff corridor obscured radar returns in the frequency bands used by "Fan Song," "Barlock" ground-control and E-band AAA radars. Often, strong winds moved or fragmented the corridors. Inside them, or above chaff blankets, no losses occurred, but only four cells probably received full protection during *Linebacker II*'s first three nights.

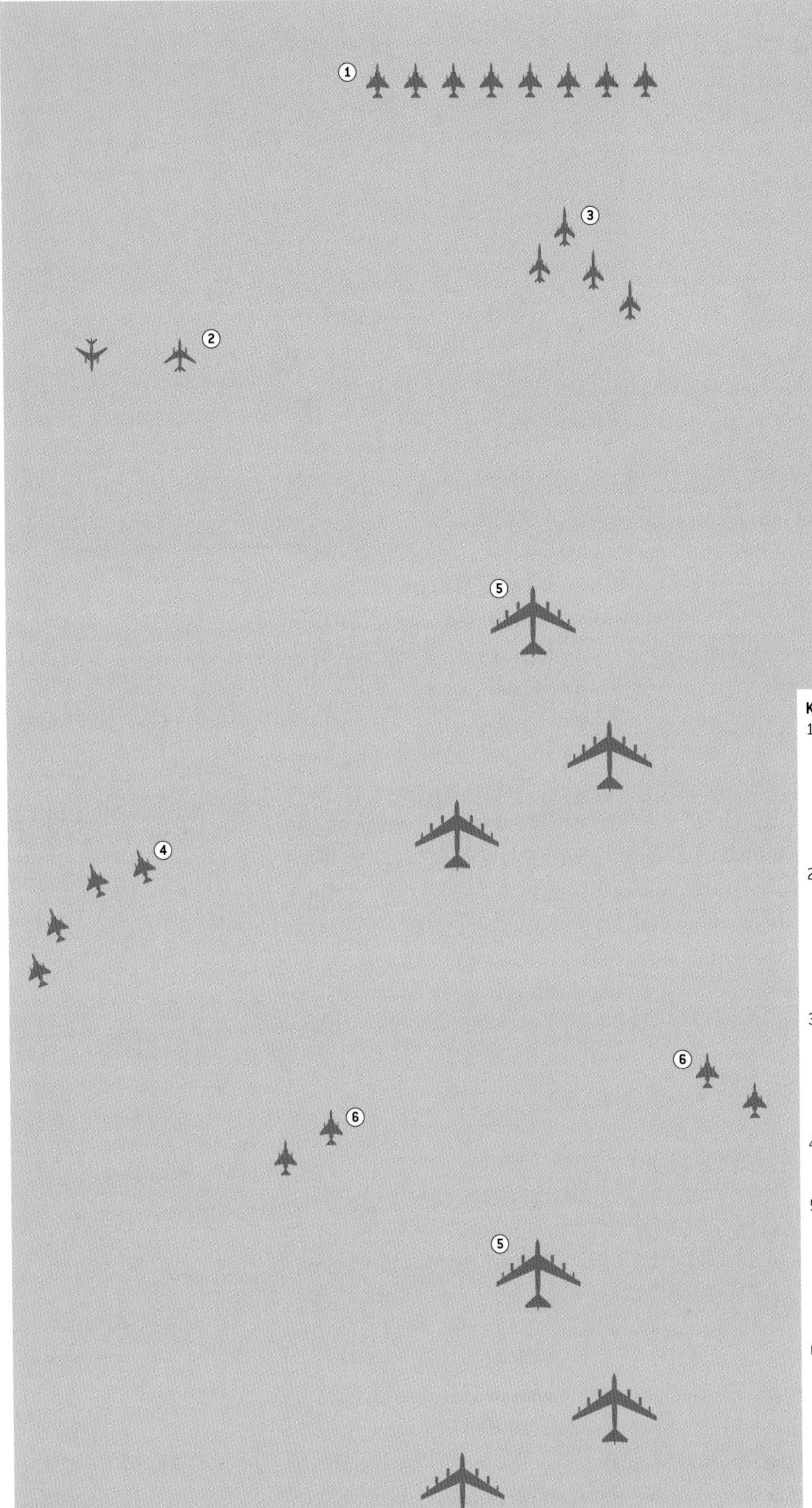

Key

1. Chaff flight of eight 8th TFW F-4Es each with nine Mk 129 chaff bombs flying ahead of the B-52s and creating a corridor up to five miles wide by 32 miles long, lasting for around 30 minutes. Up to 20 F-4 "chaffers" were used.
2. Two EB-66C/Es maintain an ECM orbit over Laos, concentrating on jamming the four frequencies utilized by P-12 "Spoon Rest" radars. Off-shore jamming support from US Navy EA-6B and US Marine Corps EA-6A was also provided.
3. *Iron Hand* flight of *Wild Weasel* F-105Gs. Up to ten were used on the first two nights of *Linebacker II*, but four A-7Es sometimes replaced one F-105G flight. F-4E bombers with CBU canisters were also used.
4. MiGCAP flights of F-4D/Es covering potential MiG routes from VPAF bases.
5. B-52D/G cells at 35,000–40,000ft, each one stepped down by 500 ft altitude between aircraft and separated laterally by about 1nm. Cells were initially around four minutes apart, reduced to two minutes on December 21/22.
6. Two-aircraft F-4D/E close escorts (many with "Combat Tree" target identification equipment) flying five miles behind each cell at 25,000ft and turning back in a racetrack pattern to escort the next cell and offer initial MiG protection for chaff flights.

For each B-52 mission, one or two flights of *Wild Weasel* F-105Gs provided vital but very hazardous SAM suppression. Their role was summarized as follows in the 388th TFW Tactics Manual:

> The actual destruction of SA-2 sites is normally of secondary importance in the suppression role, and would not normally be carried out unless a particular site could be destroyed without sacrificing the protective suppression the strike force requires from other threatening sites.

"Suppression" meant forcing "Fan Songs" to close down to avoid anti-radiation missiles. Only 23 F-105Gs were available for most of *Linebacker*, supported by six Shrike-capable EF-4C Phantom IIs. Each carried two 390lb AGM-45A/B Shrike anti-radiation missiles (ARMs) that would follow a "Fan Song" S-band signal back to its source for up to 18 miles if it was transmitting for more than 18–20 seconds, but it could not lock onto the missile's uplink signal. Its relatively small 147lb warhead usually damaged "Fan Song's" radar dish or van. The missile could be defeated by briefly using two adjacent radars, confusing its guidance.

Pre-emptive Shrike launches could force radars to shut down, and "Fan Song" took more than a minute to warm up again. SAM operator Nguyen Van Dinh told the author that, "Our soldiers recognized the dangers of the Shrike and could move the missiles to another site to avoid attack." "Fan Song" was modified by Soviet technicians to employ a "dummy load" heat-sink plug, with the radar at full power but not transmitting so that it was available at 30 seconds' notice. Technicians also learned to switch from automatic to manual "three point" tracking to overcome intense jamming. F-105Gs could carry the 15ft-long AGM-78A/B Standard ARM, which had a 215lb warhead, a 56-mile range, and a memory for locating any radar that it detected even when the system closed down. Nevertheless, its success rate was still only around 20 percent from 286 launches, and supplies were short.

SAM FIRING

SAM crews received initial training in the USSR, and the first batch of around 1,000 recruits endured six months of 14-hour daily sessions or a two-year course at Bacu army base. Nguyen Van Dinh was 18 years old when he trained to join the 275th Missile Regiment. Instruction was in Russian, and Soviet advisors accompanied them to North Vietnam for continuation training. Their service lives were hard, with primitive feeding and sleeping conditions and almost constant alert status. Many troops served throughout seven years of war with little time off-duty. The first classes began in May 1965, although early trainees had to return to Vietnam before their courses finished following *Rolling Thunder* attacks, which meant that many learned on the job. They were told by Ho Chi Minh that they must succeed in their first interception of a US aircraft, and this was realized when advisor Lt Konstantinov Mikhailovich and Lt La Ding Ti managed to shoot down an F-4C on July 24, 1965.

Ten Soviet training centers, manned by more than 2,200 Warsaw Pact missile experts, with supporting staff, were established in North Vietnam, and they became the first Vietnamese missile regiments. Russian advisors remaining with battalions had a largely advisory role by December 1972, despite there being a shortage of experienced "Fan Song" operatives that permitted only two or three per Air Defense Division. An

SAM troops head for their action stations at the double. Overall supervision by Hanoi's Air Defense Command Headquarters relied on telephone communication with the radar and missile sites and a large, transparent map to plot the bombers' positions. (via Dr. István Toperczer)

October 1972 conference at the 291st Missile Regiment analyzed B-52 jamming methods using *Arc Light* experience, and a team was sent to practice radar tracking of *Arc Light* missions. Further training on tracking, anti-Shrike tactics, and timing "Fan Song" transmissions continued into November.

Inexperienced crews learned fast, making the most successful interceptions at a range of 18–20 miles. They also learned to use several radars to triangulate and fix the approximate position and bearing of a jamming source. Some claimed that they made interceptions after watching Soviet advisors do it only once, although they clearly resented Soviet management and understandably emphasized their own achievements. Their unexpected early successes against the supposedly impregnable B-52 significantly raised Hanoi's morale.

Missiles arrived by sea from Russia or by rail from China, and they were assembled, fueled, and tested by understaffed technical battalions. Standard Soviet practice was to fire three missiles at each target, although some battalions used only one. Others opted for barrage-firing, employing missiles sometimes as "tail-chasers" that followed a target but were often diverted by chaff.

North Vietnam's SA-2s were managed by two missile regiments. The 257th Regiment controlled the 77th and 78th Missile Battalions and the 261st Regiment (replaced by the 274th, which had been hurriedly recalled from southern North Vietnam, gaining another battalion in the process), which included the 57th, 59th, 93rd, and 94th Battalions. The 72nd Battalion protected Haiphong until December 24, when it was redeployed to Hanoi.

SAM'S SONG

"Fan Song B" tracked the missile via the weapon's transponder beacon. It also continuously computed an interception trajectory or provided "auto track" automatic guidance (possible in the absence of jamming) or manual guidance, where three operators steered the radar via the SA-2's uplink and some fairly basic controls, including a "gain" knob to refine a jamming strobe sufficiently to aim an SA-2 at it.

Occupying cramped seats in the "UV" control van, the range tracker, elevation tracker, and azimuth tracker sat in a row, each with a control wheel and a radar scope to command one aspect of the missiles' guidance in "three point" (*Treokh Tochek*, or "TT") mode. Their tasks were similar, but required considerable skill and coordination to keep missiles on track within the narrow guidance beam pointing at the target, with more extreme maneuvering that could exceed its capabilities as it approached detonation point. "Half-angle elevation" allowed the missile to calculate a lead angle on the target, reducing its need to maneuver and increasing accuracy, but this was only feasible without jamming by the target.

The battalion commander had a radar scope to monitor data from an A-band P-12 "Spoon Rest" acquisition radar, with its 290-mile range, and a telephone line to headquarters. A fire-control officer and a technical officer managed the launches and marked up target details on a plotting board. SNR-75 "Fan Song A/B" used E/F-band radar (G-band for the "Fan Song C/E") and a narrow-band S-band (between 2 and 4GHz) radar to track the target, together with radio command guidance for the SA-2. "Fan Song" used sweep frequencies of more than 1,600 PRF for guidance. Mounted in a steerable rotating "PV van" cabin, its range was around 70 miles – far more than the SA-2's.

"Fan Song" was kept on standby while its tube-technology systems warmed up after warning of a raid, the launchers, meanwhile, being rotated in the approximate direction of the threat by the fire-control officer. Missile launch was initiated when "ready" lights illuminated. In "search" mode "Fan Song" acquired targets with directional cues from a "Spoon Rest" and a height-finder. It used a track-while-scan method, centering the target in azimuth and elevation scans by a trough-shaped vertical-sweep P-11 Lewis scanner and a P-12 horizontal sweep unit, mounted at right-angles to each other and operating together in "wide beam" and low PRF in search mode. They produced fan-shaped beams that overlapped, giving a ten-degree common radar "window" to track targets flying straight and level.

Uplink guidance, fuzing, and firing frequencies were transmitted to the missile's transponder from smaller P-15 parabolic antennas on "Fan Song," which could also be jammed. The "Fan Song" crew had to keep both target and missile within that

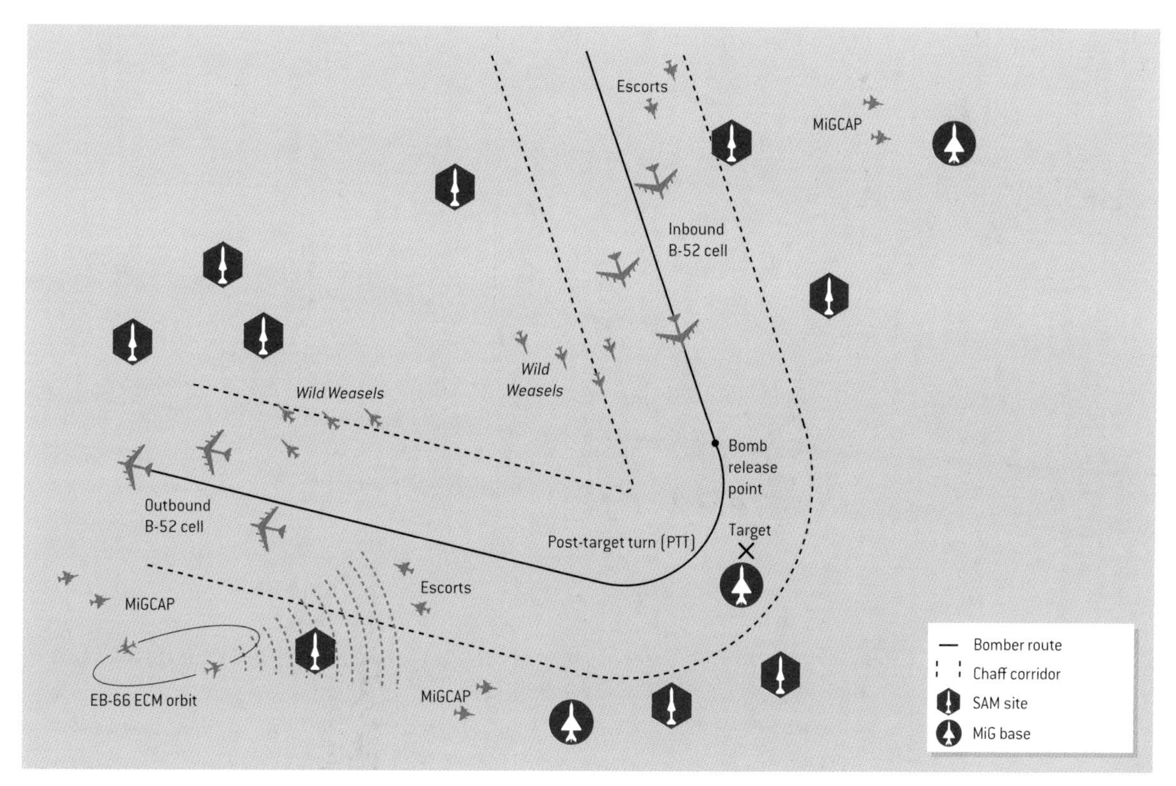

window to guide an interception within six seconds of the booster rocket section burning out and falling away, exposing the uplink antenna at the base of the missile.

For an ECM-emitting target, they would try to keep its jamming strobe image central on their displays, although heavy jamming made the screens go white. If the missile "escaped" from the window, the interception would fail and the missile went ballistic. At high altitude, where distance widened the window, it was possible to redirect the missile into a pursuit-curve interception and a "half correction" (*Polavinoye Spravleniye*) mode against maneuvering targets in which allowance was made for lead angle on the target in the initial launch, reducing major course corrections.

"Fan Song" operators' best chance was to "burn through" the ECM of B-52s or supporting 41st Tactical Electronic Warfare Squadron (TEWS) EB-66 jammers – the latter were priority targets for SAMs before B-52s assumed that unenviable position. When a B-52 was above a SAM site "Fan Song" could overpower maximum Phase V jamming sufficiently for a missile to lock-on. If a single B-52 was approached by a salvo of four or six SA-2s, its jamming power was insufficient to prevent them all from acquiring a lock-on, particularly when the "Fan Song" operators constantly shifted frequency until they could burn through and acquire target information. The S-75 system was most effective against targets directly overhead, rather than in a slant-range launch.

A pilot's best hope was to maneuver in an effort to break the lock of any missile that maintained an uplink at close quarters, although turning reduced jamming power and was impossible during the bomb-run. In a PTT the bomber's ECM shield was tilted to the outside of its turn so that SA-2 batteries situated inside the turn arc had a clear, tracked-launch opportunity. As a last resort the EWO could dispense chaff.

In automatic tracking mode, the P-11 and P-12 scanners reverted to narrow-beam to produce target angle tracking signals in azimuth and elevation using the missile's transponder beacon to make automatic course corrections, as long as the weapon stayed within the 7.5 degrees width of the beam. In the later "Fan Song E" there were also two narrow-beam P-13 and P-14 B-band parabolic transmitter antennas above the horizontal scanner. The radar changed to a high PRF and a narrow sweep using its P-13 and P-14 parabolic antennas when it had secured a lock-on to a target. "Fan Song" could acquire up to six targets but only track one at a time. It could direct three missiles at that target at once, firing them at six-second intervals, improving the probability of interception. An indicator light showed proximity fuze detonation.

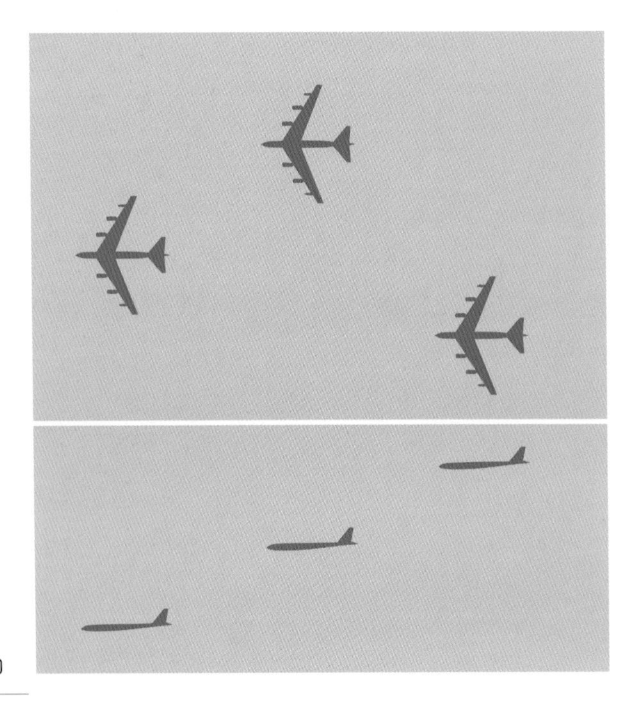

A typical *Linebacker II* three-aircraft cell formation. The bombers were separated vertically by about 500ft and horizontally by a distance of two miles between the lead aircraft and the last one in the cell.

SA-2 batteries' tactics on Night 3 of *Linebacker II* convinced a number of EWOs that a new E-band (2,000–3,000 MHz) and I-band (9,000–10,000 MHz) radar signal, coded T-8029 (or B-427Z "Teamwork") was in use. Based on ELINT from EB-66 and RC-135 aircraft, it was assumed that a "Fire Can" AAA control radar was being used, particularly at the mythical "killer site VN-549," to provide range information so that "Fan Song" use could be avoided and the missile could reach a point where its proximity fuze would operate. In fact, SAM operators were firing missiles without "Fan Song" and then using it for a few seconds to guide the SA-2 in its terminal phase. They were also switching repeatedly between low (E-band) and high (I-band) frequencies to defeat jamming. US Marine Corps EA-6A Intruders helped to jam the I-band.

In 1967, battalions attempted to track on the jamming emissions from fighter-bombers' ECM pods – a technique that proved more useful in 1972 against B-52s' jammers. They also perfected "three-point" (triangulating information from several radar sites to establish the bombers' location) and "track on jam" methods of SA-2 launching in which the "Fan Song" remained in "receive" rather than "transmit" mode and range, bearing, and altitude data was taken from "Spoon Rest" acquisition radars.

Range tracking controller Nguyen Xuan Dai was among the early recruits to the 236th Missile Regiment, the first to see combat, which was responsible for the destruction of F-4C 63-7599 of the 47th TFS/15th TFW on July 24, 1965 – the first SAM shoot-down of the war. He recalled his regiment's decoy techniques after launching missiles. They erected "fake missiles made of bamboo framework that had been painted green to resemble an SA-2. These attracted US aircraft and enabled the AAA units around the site to find the targets easily. Five American fighters were shot down while attacking these fake sites."

US tactical aircraft caused casualties too, however. Pham Truong Huy described to the author how his crew were within minutes of intercepting a B-52 in 1972 when his fellow "Fan Song" operator Kham, seated at the command computer, was hit in the head and killed by shrapnel before he could put on his steel helmet. Huy also explained that his 62nd Battalion had been responsible for the shoot-down of EB-66C 54-0466 "Bat 21" of the 42nd TEWS on April 2, 1972 shortly after moving south to Quang Tri, and that they had also claimed a B-52 in the same area.

Southerly deployments were hard on SA-2 crews, who could be away from home for up to seven years, living rough. Missile troops were awarded honors following the reunification of Vietnam, but the details of their activities and losses still remain an official secret in that country. Their motto was "*Ban Roi Tai Cho! Bat Xong Giac Lai!*" ("Shoot down the plane on the spot! Capture the pirate pilot alive!").

Douglas EB-66 Destroyers were crucial in learning the electronic secrets of the S-75 system in North Vietnam and they remained a vital part of the B-52 bombing campaign throughout the war. The 42nd Tactical Electronic Warfare Squadron (TEWS) flew about 25 aging EB-66C/E Destroyers with the primary purpose of protecting B-52 operations. No *Arc Light* B-52s were lost to SAMs or MiGs while under the protection of EB-66s. This EB-66E, 54-0440, served with the 42nd TEWS at Takhli RTAFB. In September 1970 the unit detached to the 388th TFW at Korat RTAFB, coded "JW." (USAF)

COMBAT

Having avoided SA-2s for most of the war, B-52s were committed to strategic missions during the *Linebacker II* campaign that saw them attacking targets protected by intensive, integrated air defenses rather than undertaking "tactical milk runs" over South Vietnam. Night 1 (December 18/19, 1972) of the three-day maximum effort to damage 14 North Vietnamese targets included no fewer than 300 B-52 sorties into the Hanoi area. Thirty-three 43rd SW B-52Ds, 54 72nd SW(P) B-52Gs from Andersen and 42 B-52Ds from U-Tapao's 307th BW comprised the largest heavy bomber attack since 1945. Fully loaded U-Tapao B-52Ds carried 108 bombs, while Guam B-52Ds hauled 66 M117 bombs each.

The initial revelation of the Hanoi target during the mass briefing of Stratofortress crews was met with silence, and they knew the mission was something extraordinary when they saw the base chaplains visiting the flightline for the first time. Crews realized that SAC required them to proceed regardless of SAMs and MiGs, as this was the only way the mission stood a chance of being successful. It meant that for up to 20 minutes the B-52s would be exposed to SAM sites firing weapons that had been specifically designed to destroy strategic bombers.

More than 100 USAF and US Navy support and tanker aircraft were required. *Wild Weasel* SAM suppressors with F-4E fighter-bombers and chaff flights preceded the B-52 formations, while combat air patrol F-4D/Es faced the few night-capable VPAF MiGs. Nine EB-66C/E jamming aircraft orbited 40 miles west of Hanoi, while 23 US Navy EKA-3B and EA-6A/B stand-off jammers patrolled off-shore. Finally, Seventh Fleet *Iron Hand* A-7E and A-6B Shrike launchers were also scheduled to participate.

SAC required strict formation flying to maximize each B-52 cell's main protection – its combined jamming power. Cells were routed ten miles away from known SAM sites to prevent "Fan Songs" from "burning through." Rather than their long-practiced, under-the-radar attacks at 500ft, crews flew standard *Arc Light* patterns in three waves, four hours apart, in the same direction from an Initial Point (IP) at the same altitude and speed. After bomb delivery, they made a standard "SAC break turn" (post-target right turn, used for nuclear delivery and *Arc Light*) of 50–52 degrees, exiting on the same routes. Many pilots exceeded the B-52's 60-degrees banking limit to escape SAMs.

To their amazement, they were forbidden any maneuvering between the IP and the bomb-run, where level flight was needed to stabilize the bombing computer gyros. Anti-SAM maneuvering, permitted during *Arc Light*, could now precipitate a court martial, although this rule was relaxed after two nights. PTTs headed the exiting B-52s into a 100-knot headwind and directed their jamming emissions sideways rather than downwards against enemy radars. Another unwelcome order limited the B-52s' own chaff to jamming MiGs rather than the principal SA-2 threat. Pessimistic crew members anticipated a "B-52 turkey shoot."

The Night 1 armada's first wave was launched by "Charlie Tower" (the air traffic and maintenance control team) from Andersen's five miles of parking ramps at one-minute intervals. Briefly interrupted by a volcanic earth tremor, the bombers rolled out with 120°F cockpit temperatures and 100 percent humidity, accompanied by a motor-horn chorus from vehicles lining the runway. Seconds before taxiing out, each crew belatedly received three briefcases containing details of bomb-runs, target coordinates, radar imagery, and offset points. This delayed information, normally central to the pre-mission briefing, had just arrived from SAC headquarters in Omaha, Nebraska, where the entire *Linebacker* process was micromanaged by chief planner Gen "J. C." Meyer. The plans did not allow for strong headwinds that would eat into the B-52Ds' fuel reserves, requiring extra support from Kadena's 376th Air Refueling Wing KC-135A tankers at the full extent of their range.

Late delivery of mission plans also diluted the SAM suppression effort. Because the timings could not be exactly coordinated, *Weasel* pilots sometimes had to estimate the B-52s' locations and release Shrikes pre-emptively, hoping that a "Fan Song" would engage during the weapon's flight. With only two missiles for each F-105G, their deterrent force was soon spent. Two sites were destroyed, however, and 19 more closed down temporarily.

The night's targets were the heavily defended airfields at Phuc Yen, Kep, and Hoa Lac, together with logistics repair centers at Gia Lam, Yen Vien, and Kinh No. Hanoi International Radio station, a long-awaited target, was included, although after

OPPOSITE
Transferring an SA-2 from its trans-loader to an SM-63-1 launcher (left) was clearly a very labor-intensive task, although an experienced crew needed only ten to 15 minutes to do so. Trans-loaders with their ZiL-157 tractors collected SA-2s from depots, hidden in crowded urban areas. After missile firing, the launcher was lowered and the trans-loader backed up to its front end so that the five-man loading crew could swing the transport rail (on which the missile was suspended for carriage) at 90 degrees and place it end-on to the launcher. The replacement SA-2 was then slid along the launch rail into position. (via Dr. István Toperczer)

From a B-52 cockpit during *Linebacker II* night operations, SAMs appeared as a stream of bright lights rising towards the bombers. At first there was a flash as the missile lifted off and a yellow flame trail from the booster section, followed by a brighter glow as the second stage ignited and a brilliant explosion as the warhead detonated. If the missile appeared as an unwavering doughnut-shaped image in the B-52's windscreen it meant that the weapon would detonate near the aircraft just a few seconds later. (DoD)

numerous attacks failed to silence it, F-4Ds armed with laser-guided bombs finally achieved this on 27 December.

The incoming bombers were initially detected by the P-12 radars of the 45th Radar Company near Nghe An. Its operators immediately identified the contacts as B-52s by the aura of ECM around them. The Vietnamese commander reported that the stream was heading for Hanoi.

Maj Bill Stocker, a 300-mission B-52 veteran, led the first wave from Andersen's runway. U-Tapao's attack was headed by "Snow" and "Brown" cells, a minute apart, hitting three MiG airfields near Hanoi and preceded by 14 474th TFW F-111As. Eight MiG-21MF pilots had been trained for night interception, with orders to ram B-52s (Soviet *taran* tactics) if their missiles failed, but it proved hard to engage the bombers and only 25 attempts were made in all. Tran Cung took off from Hoa Lac but could not penetrate the radar jamming. Pham Tuan also tried, getting in behind 307th SW B-52D "Brown 3."

SSgt Sam Turner, the tail gunner for "Brown 3," had already noticed "numerous SAMs coming up and exploding around us. We had our target and planned to hit it, regardless. As we drew nearer to the target the intensity of the SAMs picked up. They seemed to be everywhere." Exiting the target, they were advised of a MiG closing on them. "I picked him up on radar when he was a few miles from our aircraft. A few seconds later the fighter locked onto us. I also locked onto him. As the attacking MiG came into firing range I fired a burst. There was a gigantic explosion to the rear of the aircraft." The MiG vanished from Turner's radar scope and the fireball was witnessed by MSgt Lewis LeBlanc, confirming a kill. The VPAF, however, recorded only a damaged MiG-21.

Lt Col Bill Conlee, EWO in the last wave's leading aircraft, also noted the SAM upsurge:

> We released our weapons and had started our PTT when SAM launches were detected, visually and electronically. From the time we started our turn until about 40 miles southwest of Hanoi, we came under heavy SAM attack, employing evasive action turns. During this seeming eternity we counted approximately 40 SAMs launched in our direction. After landing, the debriefers were incredulous at the large number of SAMs that had been fired during the mission.

The 261st Missile Regiment troops eventually began to overcome the jamming that had covered their screens in white fog and confusing strobes, the chaff curtains and the distracting solo F-111A strikes. They initially attempted to locate the bombers with "Spoon Rest" search radars instead of "Fan Song," guiding the missiles manually (using range and bearing that had been plotted on the map) and tracking onto the bomber's jamming strobes to make the target appear on the "Fan Song's" tracking screens, instead of using the more accurate automatic guidance. If azimuth and distance were known, the altitude could be estimated, as B-52s always flew between 32,000 and 38,000ft. Range could be calculated by using the estimated altitude, the elevation angle of the "Fan Song's" radar beam, and the third side of the triangle, a right angle.

Firing barrages of missiles ballistically into the center of chaff corridors gave some chance that guidance could be used in the final seconds. Chaff, which screened the B-52 force for only eight minutes, may have detonated some missiles' proximity fuzes.

"Tonto" flight *Wild Weasels* managed to divert two SA-2s with Shrikes but B-52D "Lilac 03" was the first bomber to suffer. Pilot Maj Billy Lyons had already banked abruptly to avoid two SA-2s just before bomb release when a third missile fired by the 52nd Battalion exploded on "03's" left. Shrapnel shredded fuel tanks, wrecked electrical systems and instruments, and prevented bomb release. Both pilots were injured, one by glass in the eyes. Crucially, hot engine bleed air was blasting into the bomb-bay. "Lilac 03" struggled back to U-Tapao, landing with 700 holes in its airframe and a bomb-load that was too hot to touch. B-52D "Rainbow 01" was also SAM-damaged, and it too returned to U-Tapao.

B-52G 58-0201 "Charcoal 01," leading three cells against the Yen Vien railway yards, was hit by two SA-2s that had been manually guided by a 59th Missile Battalion "Fan Song" onto the bomber's jamming strobes at 34,000ft. The missiles hit just prior to bomb release at 560 knots, with a 90-knot following wind and the bomb-bay doors open. EWO Capt Tom Simpson had only picked up a 100mm AAA radar lock-on prior to the SA-2s striking the B-52.

The "Fan Song" crew – Missile Control Officer Duong Van Thuan, with Ngo Van Tu, Le Xuan Linh, and Nguyen Van Do – succeeded in hitting the forward fuselage, killing the gunner, wounding pilot Lt Col Don Rissi, and bringing the bomber down into Pho Lo's rice-fields. Capt Robert Certain (navigator) and Maj Richard Johnson (R/N) ejected, becoming the first B-52 PoWs, while Rissi and his newly appointed co-pilot Lt Bob Thomas died in the fiery fall, which was watched with horror from support aircraft, including a KC-135A piloted by Capt Certain's brother that was flying an off-shore refueling track. "Charcoal 01's" wreckage was later displayed in the Hanoi Army Museum. For the B-52's crew (S-18), this had been an extra mission, as their replacements were delayed. In "Charcoal 02," close behind, EWO Capt David Zook released three chaff bundles to compensate for the loss of mutual jamming. Other pilots made steep "illegal" turns to evade missiles.

Wave 2 included 18 Guam B-52Gs (some with upgraded ECM) and 12 B-52Ds, heading for the same targets as Wave 1. They flew 5,000ft below the exiting first wave, aware that there had been combat losses, including Maj Cliff Ashley's 58-0246 "Peach 02," in which the EWO was Lt Col Jim Tramel:

> We took off from Andersen as "Peach 01," the lead aircraft in the second wave of *Linebacker II*. After we achieved our assigned altitude we leveled off and I began to perform an equipment check. During that check I determined that one of my major transmitters was inoperative, which reduced our ability to defend ourselves and, according to the then-current procedure, we changed our position from "Peach 01" to "Peach 02."

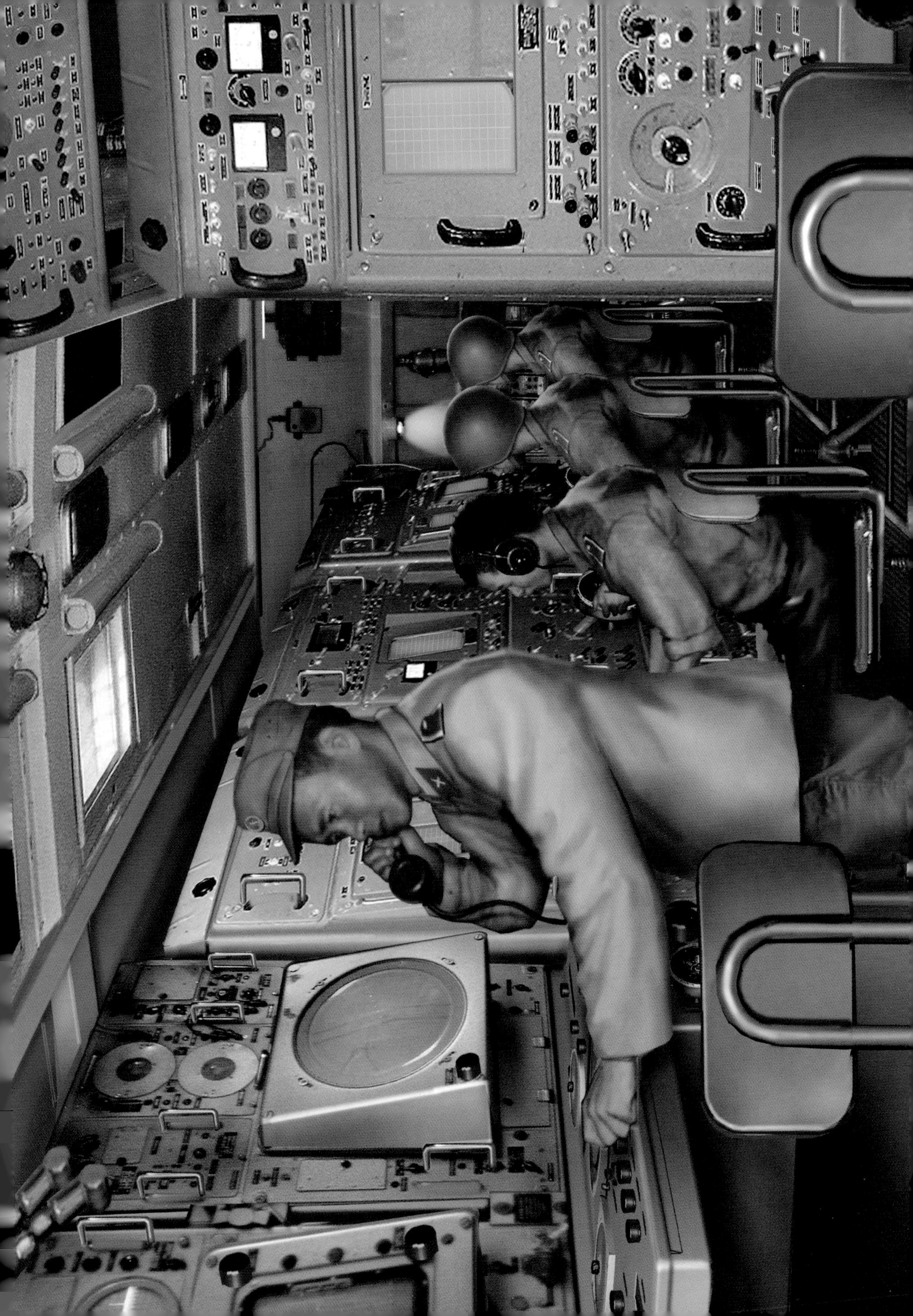

> As we left the pre-IP I began to pick up early-warning radars. During the IP run I also picked up several "Fan Song" radars. The general opinion was that the EWO should try to jam the system(s) that was the "loudest on the screen" because it was "pinging" your aircraft and probably getting ready to fire at you. In our case, I had several "Fan Song" radars on my scopes and they were all pinging the aircraft. They probably fired a barrage of SAMs at us, and I believe there were at least four SAM sites in our target area that could have fired at us. I had no way to actually verify which site fired. After our bomb drop and during the turn off the target, "Peach 02" was hit in the left wing by a SAM. The damage was enough to cause us to attempt a landing at an emergency airfield. The aircraft was a tough old bird. We flew it to the Laos/Thai border before it gave up and we had to eject.

At 38,500ft over Kinh No, the SAM blew off the external tank and started fires in two engines. Ashley turned towards Thailand without cockpit instruments, escorted by two Phantom IIs. The 2nd BW crew, including Deputy Airborne Commander Lt Col Hendsley "Hench" Connor, vacated the aircraft just seconds before "Peach 02" exploded over Thai jungle. Prior to the bomber's demise, Connor had watched the SAMs rising in his direction:

> They made white streaks of light as they climbed into the night sky. As they left the ground they would move slowly, pick up speed and end their flight in a cascade of sparkles. A beautiful sight to watch, if I hadn't known how lethal they could be. About halfway down the bomb-run the EWO began to call over the interphone that SAMs were being fired at us. We flew straight and level, and seconds later we were hit. It felt like we had been in the center of a clap of thunder. Everything went really bright for an instant, then dark again. I could smell ozone from burnt powder. The whole left wing was burning. It was a wall of red flame starting just outside the cockpit and as high as I could see.

As an extra crew member, Connor had no ejection seat, but when the navigator's seat ejected downwards it left an opening:

> The R/N turned towards me and pointed to the hole and motioned for me to jump. I climbed over some debris and stood on the edge of the hole. I looked at the ground far below. Did I want to jump? The airplane began to shudder and shake and I heard explosions as the other crewmembers ejected. I heard another louder blast. The wing was exploding. Yes, I wanted to jump!

All six men were recovered by a US Marine Corps helicopter from Nam Phong.

During the first two waves "Fan Song" operators confirmed their belief, based on *Arc Light* experience, that PTTs reduced the bombers' jamming effectiveness, giving them just ten to 15 seconds to initiate automatic lock-on and tracking. Also during bomb-runs, the B-52's huge, open bomb-bay doors greatly increased its radar signature. This weakness underlay three Night 1 losses, including the third wave's leader. Two SA-2s were aimed at B-52D 56-0608 "Rose 01's" jamming strobes near its Hanoi Radio target, which was within range of 11 SAM sites. The bomber's EWO

OPPOSITE

A "Fan Song" crew in their SNR-75 PV van manage an interception of a B-52 during *Linebacker II*. The fire-control officer (standing, left) works with the three (seated) trackers who operate their guidance wheels. From the left, they are the range tracker, elevation tracker, and azimuth tracker, supervised by the commander. The RH-1 radar scope and Plan Position Indicator are seen at the extreme left with the "Spoon Rest" radar controls immediately below them. Despite the high temperatures inside the van, protective kit was needed in case of attack by Shrike missiles or CBUs. Noisy cooling fans reduced the temperature a little, but no light could be allowed to enter in order to preserve the operators' view of their screens.

could not defeat so many radars, allowing two missiles to approach as "Rose 01" began its PTT at 38,000ft. The second SA-2 blew a large hole in the fuselage, starting numerous fires as fuel gushed into the cabin. Four crewmen immediately ejected and became PoWs, but gunner TSgt Charlie Poole (whose remains were recovered in 1996) and navigator Capt Richard Cooper went down with the Stratofortress. In another B-52D, WSO Andrew Vittoria heard the mission controller calling, "'Rose 1', 'Rose 1', please come in." There was no answer.

Night 1 had showed that repetitive attack patterns without evasive maneuvers were dangerous, but Gen Meyer's plan was set in stone. Instructions for Nights 2 and 3 arrived without changes in tactics or targets, as losses to date were considered to be within SAC's arbitrary three percent estimate. Fortunately, most missile batteries, which had fired up to 160 SA-2s on the first night, had each used up their 12 on-site SA-2s, and few replacements were ready at technical centers. Also, some had been wasted against low-flying F-111As which, from December 20, targeted SAM sites and well-hidden storage areas with CBU-58 cluster bombs, sometimes with spectacular results when missiles detonated on the ground.

As the third Night 1 wave returned, 90 B-52s for the second night were preparing to take off, led by Maj Tom Lebar. Crews picked up anecdotal information on the losses, numbers of SAMs, and the importance of mutual ECM formation, particularly for unmodified B-52Gs. Despite following Night 1 tactics, although at slightly lower altitudes and with wind-dispersed chaff corridors, most Night 2 B-52s evaded "Fan Song" tracking. Many missiles were fired, nevertheless. Col James R. McCarthy, CO of the Guam-based 43rd SW, in "White 01" reported that:

> As we turned over the IP the EWO detected the first SAM lock-on. Suddenly, the gunner broke in on the interphone to report that he had two SAMs, low, heading right for us. The EWO confirmed that they were tracking towards us. The co-pilot then reported four missiles coming our way on the right side. Added to the pyrotechnics were Shrike missiles, which would give us momentary concern until we identified them – it was nice to watch something bright streaking the other way.
>
> As we approached Hanoi we could see other SAMs being fired. As one was fired on the ground an area about the size of a city block would be lit up by the flash. This was magnified by the light cloud undercast over Hanoi at the time. As the missile broke through the clouds the large lighted area was replaced by a ring of silver fire that appeared to be about the size of a basketball. This was the exhaust of the rocket motor that would grow brighter as the missile approached. The exhaust of a missile that was fired at you from the front quarter would take on the appearance of a lighted silver doughnut. Some crews nicknamed them the "deadly doughnuts." The silver doughnuts that maintained their shape and same relative position on the cockpit windows were the ones you worried about most, because that meant they were tracking your aircraft.

Heat and vibration acting on the engine nacelle struts caused metal fatigue, requiring the Airframe Repair ("sheet metal") technicians to fix cracks and replace missing rivets after many missions. Their job was made unpleasant by the sticky black deposit ("Buff dust") all over the strut area. Frequent repairs were also carried out on the metal surfaces of B-52G "wet wing" fuel tanks due to wing flexing. The six fuel tanks inside its wing made the G-model more vulnerable to loss from hot SA-2 shrapnel. (USAF)

As the wave approached the target, AAA and MiG warnings abounded, but when the bomb-bay doors were opened many "Fan Song" lock-ons showed on EWOs' equipment. "About ten seconds prior to bombs away," Col McCarthy noted, "when the EWO was reporting the strongest signals, we observed a Shrike being fired, low and forward of our nose. Five seconds later several SAM signals dropped off the air and the EWO reported that they were no longer a threat." After releasing its 22-ton bomb-load, the B-52 began its PTT. "A second later a SAM exploded where the right wing had been. The turn had saved us." More SAMs approached, arched above the B-52, and exploded at greater altitude. "We saw another Shrike launched and again some of the threat signals disappeared. Those F-105 *Wild Weasel* troops were earning their pay that night."

Guam's Wave 2, four hours later, bombed without loss, although "Hazel 02" was struck by an SA-2. It was in fact the only B-52G to survive a SAM hit, the resulting damage from the missile causing the bomber to drift nine miles off course and knocking out its AN/ALR-20 reception.

Six U-Tapao aircraft hit the Hanoi Radio target that same night, with SA-2 operators waiting until the cell had commenced its 45 degrees PTT before establishing an automatic lock-on. "Ivory 01's" EWO detected uplinks for three missiles, one of which (from site VN-549) exploded 100ft behind their PTT. Two engines caught fire and tail control runs were cut. "Ivory 01" was in serious trouble and losing fuel fast, but Capt John Dalton's crew evaded another SAM and nursed the badly damaged B-52D back to Nam Phong RTAFB, only to lose electrical power on approach. Without stabilizer trim for a normal landing, Dalton dropped the aircraft hard, blowing two tires but stopping within the runway's length. When interviewed later about the mission's dangers, Dalton (who was awarded a Silver Star) commented, "Maybe we can get our prisoners-of-war back."

Wave 3 survived SAM barrages, which reinforced SAC's decision to repeat its tactics on Night 3, despite pleas from U-Tapao's 17th Air Division commander, Brig Gen Glenn Sullivan, for more flexibility. Minor adjustments included a narrowed entry corridor that avoided some Hanoi defenses but still overflew the 261st Regiment's missiles, which would be responsible for eight of the 15 total B-52 losses. There was also an inconclusive debate at SAC HQ about the PTT. Lt Gen Glen Martin, vice commander-in-chief of SAC, noted, "We also learned that the B-52 ECM systems needed immediate adjustment for better protection against SAM guidance radar." Tests at Eglin AFB against "Fan Song" simulators were conducted and the results, available only after the heaviest losses, confirmed that PTTs degraded B-52 jamming emissions. It was also revealed that the EWOs' radiation patterns against the SA-2's downlink beacon were ineffective as Soviet technicians had replaced the missiles' FR-15 transponders long before *Linebacker*. EWOs were belatedly told to alter their jamming patterns.

While SAC stuck to its complex plan, NVA missile regiments sought to reverse their disappointing Night 2 results and conserve missiles. A fifth assembly center was also established. Assuming that the bombers would repeat Night 3's plan, the NVA moved batteries from south of Hanoi to the northwest along the B-52s' approaches. They also emphasized the proven "track on jam" tactic, reverting to automatic guidance when the bombers were directly above with bomb-bay doors open for 30 seconds. This allowed

Capt Terry Geloneck from the 456th BW was the commander of B-52G 57-6496 "Quilt 03," which was brought down on December 20/21 1972 – Night 3 of *Linebacker II*. It was hit by two SA-2s during its post-target turn. Capt Geloneck and three other crew members became PoWs, but EWO Capt Craig Paul and R/N Capt Warren Spencer were killed. Capt Geloneck's helmet is seen here preserved in a Hanoi military museum. (via Dr. István Toperczer)

the B-52 EWOs mere seconds to initiate jamming if missiles emerged from the cloud-base at Mach 3.

Night 3's high winds dispersed chaff corridors during the bombers' 30–45-minute passage across the target area, and some SAM victims were up to 14 miles outside chaff protection. "Fan Song" operators decoyed *Wild Weasels* into firing Shrikes at radars that were briefly turned on and off, breaking the Shrikes' locks. Waiting until the first wave approached bomb release, the 93rd Battalion fired at "Quilt" cell of 72nd SW(P) unmodified B-52Gs, two of which had faulty jammers. "Quilt 03" (57-6496) was hit and destroyed during its PTT, killing EWO Capt Craig Paul and R/N Capt Warren Spencer – the remaining four crewmen were captured.

"Brass" cell came later in the procession to Yen Vien. During the PTT it lost ECM integrity when "Brass 01" moved six miles ahead of the cell, leaving crew S-02 in "Brass 02" (42nd BW B-52G 57-6481) with two inoperative jammers and unmodified ECM. Two missiles approached as the B-52 left "Brass 03" to evade other SAMs. They exploded on "Brass 02's" right, destroying four engines, hydraulic and electrical systems, and radios. With elementary dead-reckoning from his navigators, Capt John Ellinger coaxed his burning bomber across Laos for 40 minutes until the crew abandoned the B-52 near Nam Phong.

Capt Rolland Scott, in B-52G "Gold 02," flying the whole trip on seven engines, saw fiery "Brass 02" ahead and wondered how the SA-2s were achieving such accuracy when his EWO had reported no uplinks or downlinks:

> We visually detected missiles approaching from our "11 o'clock" and "one o'clock" positions. Several pairs of missiles were launched from those positions. I was extremely worried that missiles were also approaching from our rear that we could not see. They arrived in pairs, a few seconds apart. Some, as they passed, would explode – a few close enough to shake my aircraft. Apparently, a MiG-21 we saw was flying with us to report heading, altitude, and airspeed to the missile sites. During the PTT, we once again became an item of interest to the missiles. From our left and below were at least three missiles approaching rapidly. I felt I had no chance to avoid them by either maintaining or rolling out of the right turn, so I increased the planned bank angle drastically and lowered the nose. The SAMs passed above us from our left.

It was one of several life-saving, non-regulation initiatives that night.

The next two cells, "Snow" and "Grape," passed through safely, but "Orange" cell attracted MiGs and SAMs. "Orange 03," 99th BW B-52D 56-0622, was damaged by an "Atoll" air-to-air missile, starting a fire, although no VPAF claim was made. As Maj John Stuart steadied it for bomb release, the other two cell members began PTTs. The SAM battalion took advantage of the reduced jamming and "Orange 03's" enlarged radar signature and hit it with two SA-2s. Still loaded with bombs, the B-52 exploded as it went into a flat spin, killing four crewmen – Capt Tom Klomann and 1Lt Paul Grainger were captured. The bomber's flaming fall was visible for 80 miles.

An EWO in a later B-52D cell reacted to the unprecedented destruction by releasing chaff during the PTT, diverting two SA-2s that could have hit his aircraft. His pilot, Glenn Russell, made another unauthorized SAM-avoidance maneuver, and the EWO, R. J. Smith, became a popular hero by finding the frequency of the NVA's defense radio network and blowing a loud whistle over the airwaves, followed by a "Time out!" call.

The loss of three B-52s from the first wave prompted a recommendation by Seventh Air Force commander Gen John Vogt that the operation should be suspended. However, in Omaha, Gen Meyer ordered the mission to "press on," with one concession – two cells of unmodified B-52Gs (which had been targeted on heavily defended railway yards in central Hanoi) were recalled from the second wave, while 21 D-models continued onwards. Twelve B-52Gs, hitting the Kinh No complex in Wave 3 were also told to proceed so as to avoid serious force reduction.

Ironically, missile reserves were by then so low that the Wave 2 B-52Gs might have survived. The SAM battalions' successes had precluded missile rationing and two battalions north of Hanoi ran out, consequently adopting a new slogan, "one missile fired, one B-52 destroyed." Launches were reduced to 40 and two Haiphong battalions were ordered to reinforce Hanoi's defenses. Second-wave B-52Ds hitting Thai Nguyen and Bac Giang targets north of Hanoi passed through unscathed, but Wave 3 was less fortunate. Andersen lost its first B-52D when "Straw 02" (56-0669 of the 306th BW) in the second cell bombing the Hanoi railway repair workshop was hit during its PTT by one of 18 SA-2s. The 257th Regiment operators saw that it was far outside its chaff corridor and fired automatically after near-misses by other batteries. An SA-2 impacted the wing, destroying two engines and electrical systems. Leaking fuel and losing height, the B-52 staggered across Laos and crew members that ejected from the bomber were rescued by an HH-53 helicopter. However, Maj Frank Gould (R/N), wounded by the SAM, was not found.

Unmodified B-52G 58-0198 of the 92nd BW was next to fall. "Olive 01," carrying the deputy airborne mission commander, Lt Col Keith Heggen, had lost mutual ECM protection when "Olive 03" maneuvered, placing it two miles ahead of "Olive 02." Two aircraft detected a 50-second uplink signal as they approached bomb release. Tracked by seven SAM sites and lacking jamming power, "Olive 01" crashed in flames after being hit by a 77th Battalion SA-2 during its PTT. The commander, Hawaiian-born Lt Col Jim Nagahiro, Lt Col Heggen, and Capt Lynn Beens survived, although Heggen later died in captivity.

One more disaster followed. "Tan 03," another unmodified

B-52Gs (59-2572 in the foreground) fill every revetment and taxiway at Andersen. Operations on "the Rock" were controlled by "Charlie Tower," the control center in which instructor pilots with more than 2,000 hours on the B-52D/G handled up to 15 aircraft simultaneously as they taxied in an "elephant walk," took off, or experienced emergencies. At peak times about 30 bombers had to be airborne at once to create enough space at the base. Those parked in the most distant revetments had to taxi up to two miles to the active runway, which ran slightly downhill for 7,500ft and uphill for 5,000ft, ending with a 1,000ft overrun and a 500ft drop over a cliff. Updrafts from the cliff added to handling problems and two B-52Ds (56-0593 and 56-0630) hit the sea after take-off in 1969, killing 14 crew members, although the second loss also involved a fatigue failure of the starboard wing. (USAF)

While the B-52D/F gunner's position was very useful in detecting SAM threats, his direct view rearwards was through the transparent dome of his fire-control periscope sight. Many of the reported sightings of MiGs flying alongside B-52 formations were later revealed as escorting F-4s. (USAF)

B-52G (58-0169 of the 97th BW) with inoperative bombing/navigation radar, was relying on a "Bonus Deal" with "Tan 02," but "Tan 03" broke the contact and moved six miles out of the cell. It was hit by an SA-2 and reared up steeply. Although SSgt Jim Lollar ejected into captivity, the remaining five crew members died when the defenseless B-52G, with a full bomb-bay, was hit again by two more missiles and exploded as Capt Randy Craddock and co-pilot Capt George Lockhart struggled to control it.

These disturbing events were clearly visible to later cells entering the target area. Maj Dick Parrish, an R/N in "Aqua" cell, reported that:

> Both the pilot and co-pilot [Capt Chris Quill and Joe Grinder] saw a burning aircraft at a lower altitude [probably "Straw 02"]. As we pressed on I heard Chris and Joe say "Good Lord, what was that? Must have been a direct hit. My God, what a fireball!" Right after that [probably the explosion of "Tan 03"] the EWO yanked us back to our own situation by stating that his scope was covered in threat signals. I couldn't worry about the EWO's threats, or fireballs or anything else. I had only one job – to get the bombs on the target with no mistakes.
>
> As things quietened down Quill peered back and down to the left and spotted two white streaks coming at us. The next thing I knew, we were in a steep descending right turn. Almost instantly, Leo Languirand saw two traces come onto his gunnery scope. Then the two blips disappeared. We figured they went off just about where we would have been.

The final B-52s facing the six Hanoi-based missile battalions (the 77th, 78th, 79th, 88th, 93rd, and 94th) were in "Brick" cell, and Capt John Mize's B-52D "Brick 02" was near the explosion of one of their last four of 220 SA-2s. Shrapnel penetrated the cabin during its PTT, narrowly avoiding the EWO's head. The bomber returned safely to U-Tapao with 19 holes in its skin.

Although the B-52s wrought considerable destruction, the night of December 20/21 was a disastrous experience for SAC, with four unmodified B-52Gs and two B-52Ds destroyed and another badly damaged. Others survived only by making unauthorized maneuvers. Some B-52s were tracked by up to three "Fan Songs" simultaneously. The North Vietnamese felt that their SAMs were defeating *Linebacker*, persuading their delegates to walk out of the Paris peace talks.

DIVISION AND REVISION

There were many, basic proposals from aircrew for more flexible tactics to avoid crippling losses. Crews criticized the single-file bombing stream, lack of altitude separation between cells, use of only two wind-prone and route-limiting chaff corridors instead of a "blanket" over the target (a change that was delayed by a shortage of chaff), bans on chaff dispensing by B-52s and restrictions on evasive maneuvers. Above all, crews and commanders were adamant that the PTT and repeated, predictable routes needed urgent changes, and that unmodified B-52Gs should not fly over Hanoi. With so much to reconsider SAC returned Andersen-based B-52s to *Arc Light* sorties, ostensibly to give newer crews practice in cell integrity, and used U-Tapao B-52Ds for *Linebacker II* strikes.

Thirty B-52Ds hit three Hanoi airfields and storage buildings on Night 4, December 21/22. Time separation between cells was halved to two minutes, PTTs were eliminated, B-52s egressed straight out to sea and EWOs directed an extra AN/ALT-22 against "Fan Song" downlink emissions. Eighteen B-52Ds bombed successfully, but four cells attacking Bac Mai suffered badly. The missile batteries expected three waves but they tracked a single wave approaching on the usual path and expended their 70 SA-2s carefully.

"Scarlet 01" was 96th BW B-52D 55-0061 with a previous radar fault. As it turned towards the target the bombing/navigation radar failed again, and pilot Capt Pete Giroux, on his 43rd Stratofortress mission over North Vietnam, moved "Scarlet 02" into the lead and attempted to drop back in the formation (as "Scarlet 03") and seek a "Bonus Deal" B-52D. EWO Capt Pete Camerota reported numerous "Fan Song" threats against the isolated B-52D, overwhelming his jammers. A rumored MiG threat necessitated further maneuvering. Two SAMs passed nearby without exploding, but two more from another battery had been manually guided towards the bomber, switching to automatic tracking as they approached without alerting Camerota. Both detonated beneath "Scarlet 03" and the aircraft disintegrated, killing three crewmen. Giroux, gunner MSgt Louis LeBlanc and Camerota were imprisoned, although the latter spent 12 exhausting days evading capture.

A few minutes later, 7th BW B-52D 55-0050 "Blue 01" avoided ten SAMs as it neared release point. Co-pilot Capt Dave Drummond had looked ahead at the defenses and remarked, "It looks like we'll walk on SAMs tonight." Two bombers in the cell used three jammers against downlinks. As their bombs fell, "Blue 01" was simultaneously targeted by two salvoes of six SA-2s. Lt Col William Conlee reported that, "Shrapnel cracked the pilot's outer window glass, started fires in the left wing and wounded Lt Col Yuill (pilot), Lt Col Bernasconi (R/N), Lt Bill Mayall (navigator) and myself." John Yuill's crew (including three lieutenant colonels) all ejected one minute before the aircraft exploded, becoming the only complete crew to be made PoWs. It was their third mission in four days. All returned home in 1973, and Yuill's son later became a B-52 pilot.

Two further losses was another severe blow, and pressure on President Nixon to end *Linebacker* increased. However, he insisted upon prolonging it "indefinitely" until Hanoi negotiated meaningfully.

The next two nights (December 22–24) brought respite, with no losses. Targets were in the less-defended Haiphong area, with widely spaced approach and exit routes off-shore, limiting time over the defenses to a few minutes. Six approach tracks were used, some feinting towards Hanoi. Seven SAM sites were attacked by US Navy aircraft while F-4s laid a chaff "blanket." Haiphong's SAM batteries were unprepared, firing only 43 missiles, and Hanoi's regiments were convinced that they had forced the B-52s to seek easier targets.

Night 6 reinforced this belief when 30 B-52s, including 12 Andersen aircraft, hit storage areas 50 miles from Hanoi. Six Andersen B-52s diverted to bomb three SAM sites 30 miles north of Hanoi, taking them close to the Chinese border. They had to overfly the sites, increasing the chances of radar "burn through," so each site was bombed by a separate B-52, followed by a singleton in the follow-up cell, on the assumption that the missile operators normally used the first two cells to set launch parameters for later cells. PTTs were shallower and altitudes were varied within a 7,000ft range.

Fighter and *Weasel* units received the mission plans too late, and poor weather reduced support aircraft numbers. Several MiG-21s intervened, firing missiles unsuccessfully, and "Copper 03's" gunner claimed two MiG kills, both unconfirmed, but only four SAMs were seen. Hanoi leaders assumed that these more distant attacks were intended to make them disperse their SAM units.

A U-Tapao mission on Night 7 (December 24) avoided Hanoi's SAMs, using Laotian approach routes to confuse the defenses. MiG-21s appeared and 307th SW B-52D gunner Albert Moore in "Ruby 03" claimed one, denied by Hanoi. John Mize's B-52, "Purple 02" had one engine and its flying controls slightly damaged by 100mm AAA – the only instance of B-52 flak damage during *Linebacker II*, although MiG-21MF pilot Pham Tuan claimed the hit.

A Christmas cease-fire allowed much-needed crew rest, but it also enabled the defenders to re-stock and establish a ring of 12 missile batteries, including two reserve units, around Hanoi to cover all approaches. Site protection by AAA was increased, additional missile assembly lines were set up and Military Region 4's SA-2 reserves were moved to Hanoi. President Nixon, frustrated by North Vietnamese intransigence and growing domestic opposition to *Linebacker*, wanted a decisive blow immediately after Christmas. Reconnaissance revealed less bomb damage than originally estimated and Nixon calculated that Hanoi, encouraged by the B-52 losses and reduced bombing, might refuse negotiations.

The massive, 120-bomber attack on December 26 (Night 8) involved seven waves of aircraft in 40 cells hitting ten targets in the Hanoi/Haiphong and Thai Nguyen areas. It was SAC's largest-ever strike force – Nixon's hammer blow to swamp the defenses and force Hanoi's negotiator, Le Duc Tho, to resume talks.

Approaching on four routes at different altitudes and intervals, the coordinated assault was concentrated within 15 minutes, maximizing the effect of the support aircraft. Steep PTTs were avoided and two chaff blankets covered Hanoi and Haiphong, forcing many SAM crews to use three-point guidance. B-52s were allowed modest evasive maneuvering – 25-degree bank turns left and right and altitude changes of 500–1,000ft. Only two AN/ALT-28s per aircraft were directed against downlinks and the rest at track-while-scan signals and height-finding radars. Forty-five B-52Gs were given targets outside the main SAM ring, using their own chaff as necessary. No SAM sites were targeted.

Troops check the electrical connections on an SM-63-1 launcher, ready for night operations in the hope of hitting a "fat calf" (B-52). The missile's speed required constant alertness by the B-52 crew as their EWO began the deadly chess game with the enemy radar operators. For example, EWO Maj Bob Dickens, flying on December 26, 1972, announced, "Crew, EW, I have launch on two – 'one o'clock' and 'nine o'clock'. No uplink." Moments later, approaching the threat area, he added "EW has uplink" and pilot Capt Dick Purinton noticed a SAM. A barrage of missiles soon followed. (via Dr. István Toperczer)

Compressed timing minimized how long each cell spent within range of a site, giving it only one shot at the bombers. It was a belated tactic, although all *Linebacker II* formations were "compressed" compared with the timings of early *Arc Light* waves, which had seen two fatal mid-air collisions, prompting longer wave separations and cell spacing. Faultless timing and coordination were required, although a 20-minute delay in launching Kadena's tankers meant major readjustment, and gave many Andersen crews an 8,000-mile flight.

Col James R. McCarthy, in the lead for Wave 1 in B-52D 55-0680 "Opal 01," saw early, distant SAMs tracking erratically and exploding far above them. As they approached the target, the "Fan Song" signals strengthened, and he noted that:

> Capt Don Redmon (EWO) reported three very strong signals tracking the aircraft. Maj Bill Stocker ordered the cell to start their SAM threat maneuver. Then the SAMs really started coming. It was apparent this was no "F Troop" doing the aiming. As we had long learned to do, we fixed our attention on those which maintained their same relative position even as we maneuvered. All of the first six missiles fired appeared to maintain their same relative position in the windshield. Then A1C Ken Schell reported from the tail that he had three more SAMs at "six o'clock" heading for us. Out of the co-pilot's window 1Lt Ron Thomas reported four more coming up on the right side and two at his "one o'clock" position. Bill reported three more on the left as the first six started exploding. Some were too close for comfort.
>
> About 100 seconds prior to bombs away, the cockpit lit up like it was daylight. The light came from the rocket exhaust of a SAM that had come up right under the nose. The EWO had reported an extremely strong signal, and he was right. It's hard to judge miss distance at night, but that one looked like it missed us by less than 50ft. The proximity fuze should have detonated the warhead, but it didn't.
>
> It appeared in the cockpit as if they were now barraging SAMs in order to make the lead element of the wave turn from its intended course. Just prior to bombs away, the

72nd SW(P) B-52G 58-0244 returns to Andersen after a *Linebacker II* mission as a B-52D taxis out for another sortie. The December 26 launch of 78 B-52s from this location took more than two hours to get airborne. The waves advanced on the target in radio silence without formation lights. An imminent MiG threat was the only excuse for a radio call. For the defenders, the radar image of inline abreast F-4 chaff flights was a sign that B-52s would follow within about 15 minutes. (USAF)

formation stopped maneuvering to provide the required gyro stabilization to the bombing computers. Regardless of how close the SAMs appeared, the bombers had to remain straight and level. One crew actually saw a SAM that was going to hit them when they were only moments away from bomb release. The co-pilot calmly announced the impending impact to the crew. The aircraft dropped its bombs on target and was hit moments later. At "bombs away" it looked like we were right in the middle of a fireworks factory that was in the process of blowing up. The radio was completely saturated with SAM calls and MiG warnings. As the bomb doors closed, several SAMs exploded nearby. Others could be seen arcing over and starting a descent and then detonating.

"Ebony" cell received track-while-scan and uplink signals just before bomb release and "Ebony 01" applied maximum jamming against both. Moments later B-52D 56-0674 "Ebony 02" (in a two-ship cell with reduced ECM that was targeted by 30 SA-2s 25 miles south of Hanoi) was hit by four missiles. The first missile had struck the bomber's cockpit, causing explosive decompression and killing the pilot, Capt Robert Morris. The remaining crew managed to deliver their bombs, only to be hit in the left wing by a second SA-2, flipping the bomber over onto its back. EWO Capt Nutter Winbrow, who had struggled against four simultaneous SA-2s, probably died while ejecting from the disintegrating wreck. Gunner TSgt Jim Cook was trapped among his turret equipment until the fourth SAM hit severed the turret and he survived, severely injured. The remaining three members of the 449th BW crew also survived, although co-pilot 1Lt Bob Hudson was shot at and wounded as he parachuted down. Despite being hit by SA-2s, this aircraft was claimed by MiG-21MF pilot Pham Tuan.

In "Ash" cell, a two-ship formation attacking the notoriously well-defended Kinh Nho target for the sixth, and last, time, "Ash 02" detected three uplinks and the EWO, missing one jammer, directed his remaining units against the downlink and "Fan Song." "Ash 01" (B-52D 56-0584) became the other victim that night. It bombed successfully, but 50 miles southwest of Hanoi two SA-2s rose behind it and one exploded near the right side of the aircraft. Two engines caught fire, two more were shut down, the hydraulics were damaged, and severe fuel leaks began. Capt James Turner reached U-Tapao, but the bomber approached off-centerline, heading for parked aircraft. Turner made a second approach, during which the bomber's controls malfunctioned and it pitched up and cart-wheeled in flames, killing four of its Westover AFB crew, including Turner and EWO Capt Roy Tabler. Capt Brent Diefenbach, just back from an earlier mission, rescued co-pilot Lt Bob Hymel, who was trapped in his ejection seat in the burning wreckage. Gunner TSgt Spencer Grippen, wounded by the SAM, walked out of the separated tail section. Ironically, Hymel died in the Pentagon during the September 11, 2001 terrorist attacks.

"Cream" B-52D cell, bombing the Hanoi railway yards, had four SAMs launched at it after its EWOs jammed track-while-scan and uplink signals with all their transmitters, although "Cream 02" had lost two jammers. "Gold" B-52Ds, delayed by maintenance problems, arrived 20 minutes after the main assault without encountering SAMs.

Although two aircraft were lost (a 1.66 percent rate), both had contributed to a generally accurate 2,000-ton bombing effort. None of the feared mid-air collisions occurred, despite the complex route patterns, and both losses might have been avoided if composite five-ship cells had replaced the two incomplete ones. A chaff blanket covering an area of about 20 x 40 square miles gave far better protection than "curtains," despite additional SA-2 launchers. Above all, the onslaught revived peace negotiations, although Nixon decided to continue bombing to underline his determination.

On December 27/28 (Night 9), 30 B-52s from each base bombed railways, supply targets, and three SAM sites around Hanoi. Lack of Haiphong targets freed 54 Andersen sorties for *Arc Light*. Tactics echoed the previous night's, but six waves cleared each target within ten minutes. Pilots were told to use the eight glowing jet-pipe circles of the aircraft in front as an "artificial horizon" for station keeping and coordinated turns. Additional jamming support came from a "Giant Scale" SR-71A flown by Lt Col Darrell Cobb and Capt Reg Blackwell, which also gathered new data on enemy radar emitters and their frequency-shifting.

The NVA's decision to salvo SA-2s and overpower B-52 jamming was one reason for (somewhat belated) SAM-site targeting. Seventy-three SAMs were fired, including 31 against one cell, casting doubt on intelligence reports that re-supply was prevented by the May 1972 mining blockade of Haiphong Docks. Some were seen to explode after entering chaff released by B-52s during their PTT. U-Tapao B-52D 56-0599 "Ash 02's" bombs reportedly hit SA-2 site VN-243, while a missile from VN-549 hit the bomber in its PTT, wounding the pilot, Capt John Mize, who had survived a December 20 SAM explosion. Almost inverted by the blast, the aircraft lost all of its left engines and most instruments. Mize grappled with the bomber for 48 minutes – a considerable task for a wounded man. The electrical systems failed over the Thai border and the crew bailed out near Nakhon Phanom. Mize became the only SAC flyer to be awarded the Air Force Cross during the war.

The VPAF credited Pham Tuan, flying MiG-21MF 5121, with the damage. He fired two "Atoll" missiles and reported seeing flames around the bomber, but he may have engaged a later cell and probably saw "Ash 02" hit as he dived away to avoid the MiGCAP.

The final loss was "Cobalt 01" (B-52D 56-0605 from the 7th BW), hit by the last of three SAMs at 25,000ft near Bac Ninh, 15 miles northeast of Hanoi. Capt Frank Lewis and his crew – from the 320th BW – had managed to defeat two missiles that locked onto the B-52 one minute before bomb release, but the aircraft was hit by a third one when in a tight turn. Forty seconds after the aircraft was struck, and unable to drop his bombs, Lewis gave the order to eject. Although four crewmen survived to become PoWs, two were killed.

There were insufficient assembled missiles for another night's strong resistance. Hanoi, expecting bigger attacks, was forced to resume negotiations, but Nixon wanted swift certainty. Sixty B-52s set out on December 28/29, and the reduced response from many SAM sites (48 SA-2s were launched) revealed their shortages. On the final night (December 29/30), few SAMs appeared, but "Maple 03" was singled out by six, one of which exploded within 300ft. A 307th SW B-52G in the last cell sustained 117 shrapnel holes from numerous SAMs. Others were seen guiding erratically and exploding distantly, neutralized by *Weasels* and a heavier chaff blanket. Bombing ended at 0700 hrs on December 30. Hanoi celebrated that as a "glorious victory" in an "outstanding battle of annihilation." Its National Assembly approved the unique award of "Heroes of the People's Armed Forces" to the missile battalions.

OVERLEAF

B-52D 56-0605 from the 7th BW, attached to the 43rd SW(P) at Andersen AFB, was "Cobalt 01" on the night of December 27/28, 1972. The target was the railway marshalling yards at Trung Quang, near Hanoi, and "Cobalt" was the second of three cells attacking it. In all, 60 B-52s in six waves streamed in on five routes to attack seven targets simultaneously, regrouping as a single wave to leave the area. Precise timing and positioning were crucial. SAM sites were among the targets, including the hated "Killer Site" VN-549 that was supposed to have downed several B-52s. "Cobalt's" wave was met by 45 SAMs as it approached Hanoi. "Cobalt 01's" pilot, Capt Frank Lewis, evaded two, but a third hit the bomber in its forward wheel-well as he tried to return to level flight seconds before bomb release. R/N Maj Jim Condon (veteran of more than 120 B-52 missions) was unable to release the bombs and Lewis ordered the crew to eject, but navigator Lt Bennie Fryer and EWO Maj Allen Johnson had been fatally injured by the explosion. The remaining crew ejected into captivity, leaving gunner MSgt Jim Gough, with no intercom, in his turret. As flames streamed past, he leapt out into the night, surrounded by burning debris. VN-549 escaped the bombs and shot down B-52D 56-0599 "Ash 02." These two aircraft were the last D-models to be lost during *Linebacker II*. "Cobalt 01" was also one of the B-52s claimed shot down by VPAF pilots, in this case by Vu Xuan Thieu, whose MiG-21 allegedly rammed the bomber and was apparently fatally damaged by debris from it, crashing with its pilot near the wreck of the Stratofortress.

STATISTICS AND ANALYSIS

Arc Light missions were flown from June 18, 1965 until August 15, 1973. In 126,615 B-52 sorties more than three million tons of bombs were dropped, but only six percent of them in the North, where the decisive *Linebacker II* campaign absorbed less than one percent of the B-52s' wartime sorties. The five stages of Operation *Bullet Shot* took 57 B-52Ds to war between February and April 1972, and 91 B-52Gs were added between April and June 1972. In *Linebacker II*'s 729 sorties, B-52s dropped 15,237 tons of bombs. U-Tapao delivered more than half the total ordnance with less than a third of Andersen's B-52 numbers and flew twice as many sorties as Andersen's bombers, which undertook the majority only on December 18 and 26. The logistics for the Thai base were easier to plan. No tankers were needed for the shorter flights, allowing increased bomb-loads, and turn-around times were reduced.

B-52 support from Seventh Air Force tactical aircraft was concentrated and efficient despite repeatedly short notice of SAC's plans and requirements, and limited numbers of tactical assets. Their numbers increased from 39 on Night 1 to 113 at the height of the operation, including brand new US Navy EA-6B Prowlers to jam "Spoon Rest" early-warning radars, although they were less successful against "Fan Songs" mainly because the B-52s' own jammers blocked their AN/ALQ-99 ECM equipment in the 2,900–3,200 MHz frequency range! However, as EA-6B pilot and VAQ-132 CO, Cdr E. F. Rollins, pointed out, one B-52 wave delivered as much ordnance as 27 US Navy "Alpha" strikes, each of which could involve an entire carrier air wing (CVW). Rollins' unit was embarked in USS *America* (CVA-66) as part of CVW-1, the aircraft carrier conducting combat operations from the Gulf of Tonkin throughout *Linebacker II*.

For targets near or beyond the North Vietnamese border, *Wild Weasels* were vital companions, although mutually effective tactics took time to evolve. A SAC planning team from the two B-52 bases met *Weasel* crews from Korat RTAFB in October 1972 to discuss coordinated operations, but as Col Mike Chervenka recalled:

> We recommended they vary their altitudes, don't fly single file, and use some of the advanced features of their on-board ECM. Their answer was "no, no and definitely no." I think that not only were the North Vietnamese missile crews triangulating on the targets, but they knew the B-52 routine – so many seconds after the lead aircraft, with such-and-such an altitude separation, comes No. 2, then after so many more seconds and at slightly higher stacking comes No. 3. They were always at the same altitudes, airspeed, and separation. It was a simply "one potato, two potato, fire!"

When *Linebacker* began the North Vietnamese heartland was defended by around 145 MiGs and 26 SA-2 sites. Active SAM sites were not included in the target list issued by the JCS on December 15, 1972, although the Pentagon had already attributed the loss of 185 fixed-wing aircraft to SA-2s since 1965 compared with 87 to MiGs. There were 18 B-52 wartime combat losses and 13 to operational causes. Many of the latter could be attributed to heavy operational use of aging airframes. Ninety-two of the 1,300 crewmembers involved in the operation were in the 15 downed *Linebacker II* B-52s, 66 of them being killed or captured from the ten bombers that crashed in North Vietnam. Twenty-six were rescued.

On the worst night, December 20/21, there was a seven percent attrition rate, and the overall rate for 11 nights was 3.7 percent. SAC's arbitrary worst-case forecast was three percent, but JCS expected five percent, or 36 B-52s. While this was still a small proportion of the 3,237 US fixed-wing aircraft losses between 1965 and 1973, the symbolic effect of sustained Stratofortress losses would have been immense.

Four B-52Gs were destroyed and nine crew members were killed on December 20/21, but fewer than 300 bombs were delivered by the lightly loaded G-models, which flew 225 sorties during the 11-day onslaught. The lack of upgraded ECM provision in five of the six lost B-52Gs was a major cause of their losses. Two B-52Ds with better ECM also went down, but many others were fortunate to escape with shrapnel "wounds" from up to 200 SA-2s.

Although the massive bomb tonnage caused severe damage to targets such as the Gia Lam railway and electricity generators, post-war analysis revealed that bombing achieved less than 25 percent of the anticipated damage and scored under a third of the intended circular error probability (CEP). B-52s could hit large targets with significant radar signatures, and the rail network, a principal means of transporting SAMs from China, offered appropriate targets, as did trans-shipment points in Hanoi, Bac Giang, Lang Dang, Yen Vien, and Thai

Seen on display in Hanoi's Lenin Park in 1994, these long-retired SA-2s have been effectively camouflaged by nature. The NVA was concerned that its missile storage warehouses would be located and destroyed, but they were well dispersed, often in off-limits civilian areas, and hard to detect from the air. Some SA-2 sites were bombed by B-52s from December 26, 1972, but only with "iron" bombs rather than cluster bomb units, which were more effective against the wide spread of vehicles on a site. (via Dr. István Toperczer)

Nguyen, which attracted 269 B-52 sorties – far more than any other targets. Lang Dang (near the Chinese border) alone required 86, making it the most heavily bombed target in *Linebacker II*, while only 42 aircraft attacked the Phuc Yen SAM support facility.

In 1972 the B-52D's accuracy over urban areas could result in CEPs of around 1,000ft, although the B-52G had more precise bombing/navigation equipment. The risk of civilian casualties limited B-52 attacks on smaller military objectives within the cities, but consistently poor weather also prevented precision attacks by laser-guided weapons from F-4 Phantom IIs

Crews were told not to release bombs without certainty of the target, but to "press on" with the mission even if loss of an engine caused them to fall behind. Ninety-four percent of the force succeeded in delivering ordnance.

An off-limits target was hit when a SAM-threatened B-52D maneuvered just before its release point, bombed four seconds late, and damaged Gia Lam International Airport terminal and runway. North Vietnam's propaganda focused on Night 4 when bombs from SAM-damaged, uncontrollable B-52D "Blue 01" fell on Bac Mai hospital, from which the patients had been evacuated. In a few cases the distracting effect of SA-2s may have caused misdirected bombs, but generally B-52 crews showed remarkable fortitude in holding their aircraft steady and straight for more than five minutes during heavily opposed bomb-runs.

Avoiding civilian areas was a main priority. SAC's inappropriate tactics on the first three nights eased the defenders' task, possibly at the expense of Hanoi's civilians when SAM and AAA debris fell on them. Most were evacuated before mid-December, possibly in response to leaked information about US plans for a major offensive. Civilian losses were around 1,300, and there was minimal damage to Hanoi, although the US press presented a very different picture.

Before *Linebacker*, many B-52 crews were unfamiliar with the in-depth capabilities of North Vietnam's defense systems, and SA-2 regiments lacked experience of B-52 tactics. Hanoi claimed that SA-2 batteries were helped by technical data captured from shot-down EWOs or crashed B-52s. Soviet advice to SAM operators to overwhelm B-52's ECM through multiple launches at single aircraft to beat the EWOs was effective, although their chief advisor, Soviet Col-Gen Khypenen, was unimpressed by some of the SAM results:

> Missile crews were inadequately trained to fight when jammed and under aerial attack. Fearing anti-radar missile strikes, the launch crews tried to fire at the B-52s without turning on their radars at all, which prevented them from detecting targets under jamming and switching to manual guidance.

He estimated that only three B-52s were hit by actively guided SA-2s (in most cases by two or more missiles) and 64 missiles exploded too far from their targets, some of them in chaff clouds. As for the B-52 countermeasures' relative success, Lt Col Jim Tramel was, "frankly not sure that the EW operators' level of experience was the primary cause of whether or not an aircraft was shot down. Other factors such as the type of equipment on board, the plane's location in a cell and wave, or just being in the wrong piece of airspace at the wrong time should be included."

B-52 pilots realized on Night 1 that they had to disobey orders by maneuvering to defeat SAMs, thereby compromising ECM cell integrity. More flexible and far-reaching improvements were allowed from Night 3, and some mission planning was moved from Omaha to Andersen AFB after Night 4. Issues such as the composition of cells if one aircraft aborted or lost its jammers were debated. Should cells close up as five-ship units for stronger ECM protection or fly as a pair? SAC had not envisaged five-aircraft cells, so for several missions B-52s flew in vulnerable pairs. From December 27 five-ship cells were allowed. While SAC took time to adapt its tactics after mounting losses, NVA missile regiments were quick to devise effective responses. B-52 crews believed that SAM operators tracked the first cells of a formation to ascertain height and speed and then fired at the second and subsequent cells, but sometimes leading cells were targeted. Many B-52 crews felt that they were required to open bomb-bay doors too early, prolonging their increased radar signature.

North Vietnamese troops survey the wreckage of an unidentified B-52, shot down during *Linebacker II*. (via Dr. István Toperczer)

After Night 2, when no B-52s were lost, SAM battalions changed tactics to concentrate their fire on the bombers at their most vulnerable points – the stable bombing run with open bomb-bay doors and the PTT. They had known of this weakness in the B-52's ECM protection since shooting down Capt Ostrozny's B-52D on November 22. PTTs negated the B-52 jammers' effect for up to two minutes, allowing "Fan Song" a few seconds to acquire its target. This period of vulnerability was also known to SAC planners, who, nevertheless, favored using PTTs as it was the quickest way to exit the target area.

ECM was still such an arcane and classified business that some crew members were unaware that the PTT directed their jamming emissions at the horizon rather than protecting them from below. One crew on Night 3 foiled an imminent attack during their PTT by quickly leveling out and redirecting their jammers at the threat. Making PTTs into the frequently encountered headwind could reduce speed from 600 knots to just 350 knots, giving the SA-2 crews longer to achieve a lock-on. Missile batteries also resorted to barrage firing, using approximations of the targets' altitude to fuze the missiles' warheads – a technique which their Russian advisors found wasteful.

Losses on the first three nights forced SAC to re-think its approach, even though the momentum of the complex operation already had Night 4's B-52s lined up and ready to go with little change in the mission plan, although six of the nine B-52 losses thus far had occurred during a PTT. America's crucial nuclear deterrent was under threat, as most of the nuclear alert B-52Gs were committed to *Linebacker*, so Gen Meyer had to remove them from the Hanoi area after Night 3. SAC crews had not anticipated such losses. They were angered when Meyer and his Director of Operations, Maj Gen Pete C. Sianis, visited Andersen and, when publicly challenged by a B-52D pilot, offered no explanation for the unchanging tactics devised by a hardworking SAC team that was simply too far away from the action. Morale at both bases was eroded, although only one U-Tapao crew member refused to continue flying.

The insistence upon leaving long gaps between B-52 waves on the first four nights to minimize collision risk was misjudged, as it allowed the SA-2 batteries time to re-load. So too was the official ban on dispensing chaff against SA-2s. When this was relaxed for the final four nights, SAMs were seen to explode in the chaff clouds. On December 26, Eighth Air Force planners (keeping closer to Lt Gen Johnson's August 1972 proposals) were allowed by Gen Meyer to concentrate 120 B-52s into one massive 15-minute assault from four directions, and the results were as they probably should have been on earlier nights. Even then, SAC continued to issue last-minute, contradictory revisions to the plans.

Complex attack patterns, in which aircraft crossed over each other at different altitudes above the target, required extremely accurate timing and bomb-release coordination. Cells were closely spaced to maximize jamming power, but any aircraft that could not maintain altitude had to leave the formation to avoid risk of collision, exposing it to an increased SAM threat. However, the SA-2 battalions were undoubtedly overwhelmed and generally unable to track targets or launch missiles effectively.

Thirteen sites were attacked, with up to three sorties each within the two percent of B-52 and F-111 sorties targeted against them, but only two sites received up to 50 percent damage and eight others were slightly damaged. However, the concentrated B-52 raid on Phuc Yen SAM depot, located by SR-71 photography, on December 28/29 produced numerous secondary explosions. Strikes on SAM storage warehouses at Quinh Loi, in Hanoi, were made by LORAN (long-range navigation) F-4Ds and US Navy A-7Es on December 28, severely reducing missile supplies pending replenishment by road from China. The rural SAM support facility at Trai Ca was also hit by B-52s that same day. Only 25 SAMs were launched on December 29.

SAC's ECM experts, who had over-estimated the effectiveness of B-52 ECM, had to adapt to Soviet improvements to North Vietnamese SA-2 technology and tactics. The enemy's ability to stay one step ahead on many occasions, without introducing radically new equipment, made the EWOs' job much harder too. Reports circulated concerning unjammable "black SAMs" and "killer" Soviet-manned SAM site VN-549, equipped with I-band "Team Work" radar that was supposedly immune to the B-52G's ECM. Most of the B-52 losses were in fact attributed to two SAM units, the 57th and 77th Battalions, using standard "Spoon Rest" and "Fan Song" equipment, but their use of the latter's less familiar frequencies probably generated many rumors and required some cracking of new command codes and frequencies by US Navy cryptologists.

Gen Meyer expressed disappointment with the *Wild Weasels'* inability to stop SAMs in greater numbers, despite their heroic efforts performing the world's most dangerous job at that time. Their cluster bomb strikes were often effective, accounting for 15 sites, while B-52s' iron bombs were credited with 50 percent of one site, two others having been vacated before the bombs fell. Soviet sources asserted that 15 missiles, nine launchers, and various support vehicles were destroyed by bombing and Shrikes

High-scoring fighter ace Gen John C. Meyer, who claimed aerial victories in both World War II and the Korean War, became the seventh commander-in-chief of SAC on May 1, 1972. He and his staff officers became unpopular with frontline B-52 crews in-theater due to the traditional, rigid SAC tactics they forced crews to stick to despite mounting losses to VNA SA-2s during *Linebacker II*. Meyer retired on July 1, 1974 and died of a heart attack on December 2, 1975, aged 56. (USAF)

during *Linebacker II*, temporarily closing down six battalions. "Fan Song" use was often avoided to negate Shrikes, so the missile's deterrent effect was probably its main strength, with 160 reported shut-downs of hostile emitters after Shrike launches.

The USAF's *Corona Harvest* report said *Weasels*, "limited the enemy's use of radar, thus reducing the number of missiles he could launch with accuracy and causing a decline in the likelihood of SAM kills." Shrike was disadvantaged by its own rocket exhaust emissions, which contained metallic fragments that could be detected by radar, giving adequate warning to shut down a "Fan Song." Difficulty in locating "Fan Song" emissions was actually due mainly to their operators' skilful limitation of their radar emissions to brief periods during the B-52s' most vulnerable moments over the target. Locating and firing anti-radiation missiles at radars after such fleeting exposures was extraordinarily hard, yet there were numerous F-105 *Wild Weasel* successes.

North Vietnamese records suggest fewer than 266 SA-2 launches during *Linebacker II*, contrasting with much higher estimates from U-2R and B-52 observations. Intelligence officers required B-52 pilots and gunners to count the SAMs they saw. Multiple sightings of the same missiles may have produced inconsistent figures, but US Intelligence calculated that at least 882 SA-2s were fired during the 11 nights. Based on the figure of 882, and 24 confirmed hits on the 15 downed B-52s, the overall kill rate is less than 1.8 percent in a scenario where the bombers often presented near-perfect targets to the SA-2 system.

Analyst Steven J. Zaloga calculated that North Vietnam was supplied with 95 S-75 batteries (of which 56 were destroyed) and a total of 7,658 SA-2-type missiles, of which 5,804 were expended in action, including 266 in 1971 and 1,135 in 1972, against aircraft targets. In the latter year he judged that 27.8 missiles were needed for each of 73 aircraft (of all types) shot down, a percentage kill rate of 6.4 for the whole of 1972. Even the most conservative estimates indicate that US ECM and SAM suppression during *Linebacker II* operations were generally effective, although the SA-75MK/"Fan Song B" system used by the NVA was an early version that was susceptible to ECM. However, the 73 shoot-downs achieved by SAM batteries in 1972 was their highest total, which exceeded their next best "score" of 62 aircraft in 1967. The presence of SA-2s necessitated a hugely elaborate SEAD effort, and the installation of ECM equipment in B-52s took up considerable internal space and added extra weight to the already heavy bomber.

North Vietnamese propaganda presented the 11-day onslaught as a "Dien Bien Phu of the skies" and a victory for the SAM regiments that ended the myth of the B-52's invincibility, united the nation, and forced the Americans to abandon the war. For the communists, the spurious peace agreement merely bought time to plan their long-awaited takeover of the south unopposed by the USA. To some American leaders, *Linebacker II* was somewhat belated proof of the successful application of air power to settle political conflicts. Gen Russell Dougherty, SAC commander from 1974–77, judged that it "attacked, destroyed or neutralized almost all ground installations of military and strategic value in the Hanoi-Haiphong area" without doing significant damage to civilian areas. Nixon appeared to have achieved his aim of "peace with honor," but for many Americans the campaign's main achievement, and justification, was the repatriation of 591 US PoWs and the end of their nation's involvement in Vietnam.

AFTERMATH

The SAC badge still remains bright on the wreckage of B-52G "Charcoal 01" as a North Vietnamese guide describes its loss on December 18, 1972 to a student audience. (via Dr. Istvn Toperczer)

Although *Linebacker II* had convinced North Vietnam that it should negotiate to avoid further destruction and loss of support from its allies, the B-52 operation continued after the 11th night. By that time consistently successful tactics had been established and the bombers could have attacked any Hanoi target virtually unopposed. Nevertheless, another 307th SW B-52D, 55-0056 "Ruby 02," was shot down by a four-SAM barrage on January 3, 1973 over Vinh as it released its 500lb bombs. One devastated the cockpit, cutting engine controls. Fuel cascaded into the navigators' compartment, causing chemical burns to Capt Myles McTernan and Maj Roger Klingbeil. Three more SA-2s exploded nearby.

Fearful that operating any switches or ejection seats would spark an inferno, Lt Col Jerry Wickline and co-pilot Capt Bill Milcarek nursed the "flying bomb" out to sea at just above stalling speed, and the Dyess AFB crew,

Displayed on a supporting framework, the wrecked fuselage of B-52G 58-0201 "Charcoal 01," including other Stratofortress parts, dominates the Hanoi Army Museum. (via Dr. István Toperczer)

including EWO Capt Bill Fergason, ejected near Da Nang. McTernan's downward-ejecting seat jammed in the escape hatch, leaving him alone in the crippled, blazing bomber. Unperturbed, he extricated himself, found a spare parachute, and leaped out, landing semi-conscious with head injuries amid 15ft waves with no life-raft or survival equipment. All were eventually rescued, but McTernan, miles from the other crewmen, had to wait hours before a Cessna O-1 pilot happened to notice him.

Another B-52D (55-0116) was badly damaged during a January 13 *Arc Light* and was scrapped at Da Nang. It was the last of 31 wartime Stratofortress losses to all causes.

After the fall of South Vietnam in April 1975, the last 307th SW B-52s had left U-Tapao by June 8. Post-war, SAC presented somewhat optimistic official views of *Linebacker II* that sidelined most of the tactical errors and the criticisms from crews.

A year later some surviving B-52Ds began to appear in desert storage at Davis-Monthan AFB, Arizona. Others were proof-tested in Project *Pacer Plank* to assess their combat fatigue and select the best 80 airframes for extensive refurbishment. B-52Gs required more thorough rebuilding and a redesigned wing structure. In the 1980s, B-52Ds armed with pylon-mounted GBU-15 laser-guided bombs and all remaining B-52Gs received electro-optical television and infra-red sensors for operations without visual reference to the world outside. A much improved Phase VI *Rivet Ace* ECM program had also been initiated in 1973 for B-52G/Hs, leading to the sophisticated Offensive Avionics System in the 1980s.

In the USSR, design of a faster, longer-ranging SA-2 version, the S-75M *Volkhov*, had commenced in 1958, and it entered service as the 20D in 1961. Radically different ramjet-powered variants were tested, eliminating the heavy oxidizer fuel component of the rocket-powered version. A nuclear-tipped variant was also designed. For target guidance, it relied on the upgraded RSN-75V "Fan Song C/D/E" with shorter wave-lengths to track six targets simultaneously, a moving target indicator to defeat chaff, superior target resolution to North Vietnam's "Fan Song B/F" versions and better ECM resistance.

There was also awareness that the USA could soon produce a supersonic bomber (the XB-70 Valkyrie) that would challenge the S-75 system. To counter this threat, the low-altitude, I-band S-125 (SA-3 "Goa") entered service from mid-1961 and the high-altitude S-200 Angara (SA-5 "Gammon") appeared in 1967. Luckily for B-52 crews, the USSR could not provide North Vietnam with the S-125 during *Linebacker II* as NVA personnel were still in training on the system. The Soviet Union eventually terminated the deal, worried that China would appropriate and copy SA-3s that were delivered via the Chinese railway system. A development of the SA-2, "Goa" was more effective at lower altitudes, particularly against maneuvering targets. S-75 batteries continued to protect the Soviet bloc until the automatic Almaz-Antey S-300P Volkhov (SA-10 "Grumble") entered service in 1981. However, S-75s remained operational with many countries into the 21st century.

B-52s and SA-2s dueled again in Operation *Desert Storm* in Iraq in 1991 when up to 85 G-models flew three percent of Coalition combat missions but delivered more than 35 percent of the total bomb tonnage. Heavy AAA and SAM opposition from SA-2s, SA-3s, and SA-6s was encountered on many missions, without combat losses, although several B-52Gs were damaged by missiles. Radar suppression aircraft neutralized much of the threat.

Stratofortresses are still valuable weapons in USAF Global Strike Command's triad of B-1B Lancers, B-2A Spirits, and B-52Hs. Their increasing use of stand-off cruise missiles and precision-guided munitions, together with upgraded ECM, has minimized their exposure to ground-to-air missiles. The USAF called 2012 "The Year of the B-52," celebrating 60 years in which the Boeing bomber had become the foremost symbol of American power projection. Six years later, B-52s are still being deployed for combat. They have participated in at least eight major conflicts, including Iraq, the Balkans, Afghanistan and, most recently, against ISIS insurgents in the Middle East. The Stratofortress remains America's "big stick" during periods of international political tension, including 2017 disputes with North Korea. Progressive updates to B-52H engines and ECM could keep the aircraft credible until 2055, so that a 2017 pilot's judgment that flying it is "like driving your grandfather's old Cadillac" could add a generation to that statement.

Linebacker II veterans went to war again in January 1991, facing Iraq's sophisticated but rapidly degraded air defense network during Operation *Desert Storm*. B-52G 58-0194 *BUFFASAURUS* of the 1708th BW takes off from King Abdul Aziz International Airport at Jeddah, in Saudi Arabia, on one of its 47 *Desert Storm* missions with a Vietnam-type bomb-load. By that time the use of automatic ECM equipment allowed the EWO to manage his systems rather than operate them manually. (DoD)

FURTHER READING

BOOKS

Boyne, Walter J., *Boeing B-52 – A Documentary History* (Schiffer Publishing, 1994)
Davies, Peter E., *Osprey Duel 35 – F-105 Wild Weasel vs Sa-2 "Guideline" SAM* (Osprey Publishing, 2011)
Davies, Peter E. and Thornborough, Tony (with Tony Cassanova), *Boeing B-52 Stratofortress* (The Crowood Press, 1998)
Davies, Steve, *Boeing B-52 Stratofortress Owner's Workshop Manual* (Haynes Publishing, 2013)
Dorr, Robert F. and Peacock, Lindsay, *B-52 Stratofortress – Boeing's Cold War Warrior* (Osprey Publishing, 1995)
Eschmann, Karl L., *Linebacker* (Ivy Books, 1989)
Ethell, Jeff and Christy, Joe, *B-52 Stratofortress* (Ian Allan Ltd, 1981)
Harder, Robert O., *Flying from the Black Hole* (Naval Institute Press, 2009)
Harten, Don, *Collision Over Vietnam* (Turner Publishing, 2011)
Hobson, Chris, *Vietnam Air Losses* (Midland Publishing, 2001)
Hoopaw, James, *Tall Tail Tales* (AV8R, 2005)
Jenkins, Dennis R. and Rogers, Brian, *Boeing B-52G/H Stratofortress* (Aerofax Inc, 1990)
Kozak, Warren, *LeMay* (Regnery History, 2009)
Lacklen, Jay Lt Col, *Flying the Line* (Two Harbors Press, 2013)
Lake, Jon, *Osprey Combat Aircraft 43 – B-52 Stratofortress Units in Combat 1955–73* (Osprey Publishing, 2004)
Lake, Jon, *Osprey Combat Aircraft 50 – B-52 Stratofortress Units in Operation Desert Storm* (Osprey Publishing, 2004)
Michel III, Marshall L., *The 11 Days of Christmas* (Encounter Books, 2002)
Novak, Paul, *Into Hostile Skies – An Anthology* (Paul Novak, 2013)
Stanley, Roy M., *Chasing SAM* (Dog Ear Publishing, 2016)
Thompson, Wayne, *To Hanoi and Back* (USAF/Smithsonian Institution Press, 2000)
Yenne, Bill, *B-52 Stratofortress* (Zenith Press, 2012)
Zaloga, Steven J., *Osprey New Vanguard 134 – Red SAM: The SA-2 Guideline Anti-Aircraft Missile* (Osprey Publishing, 2007)

DOCUMENTARY SOURCES

Air War Vietnam Plans and Operations 1969–1975 (USAF Historical Research Centre/Defense Lion Publications, 2012)
Electronic Countermeasures in the Air War against North Vietnam, 1965–73 (B. Nalty, Office of Air Force History/ Defense Lion Publications 2013)
Frisby, J. E., Col, USAF (Ret), *Stuck in Las Vegas* (unpublished manuscript)
Gradual Failure, The Air War Over North Vietnam 1965–66 (Jacob Van Staaveren/Air Force History and Museums Program)
Linebacker II, A View from the Rock (USAF Southeast Asia Monograph Series, 1979)

INDEX

References to illustrations are shown in **bold**.

Aikou, fighting for 58, **59**, 60, 69
air power/support (Jpn) 20, 24, 25, **25**, 36, 37, 38, 39, 40, 44, 48, 53, 55, 56, 57, 62, 63, 66, 73, 74
armour (Jpn) 30, 34, 36, 39, 49, 57
  tankettes/tanks 21, 33, 34, 35, 36, 37, 38, 48, 53, 56, **57**, 62
artillery pieces: (Chi) 17–18, 22, 24, 30, 40, 47, 53, 72; (Jpn) 17, 22, **22**, 27, 30, 33, 39, 40, 44, **47**, 49, 54, 56, 57, 58, 62

bayonets: (Chi) **10**, 49, 67; (Jpn) 12, **14**, 21, **61**, **67**
Beijing, fighting for 5–6, 28, **28**, 29, 30, **31**, **34**, 35, 37–38, 40, 71

Central China Expedition Army 6, 56, 57
  artillery regts 61, 63
  corps 56, 57, **59**
  infantry bdes 58, **59**, 62
  infantry dvns 6, 57, 58, **59**, 60, 61, 63, 69
Central Army 8, 9, 16, **17**, 41, 55, 71, 77
  'Germanized' dvns 9, **9**, 16–17, 53, 56, **61**, 71
chemical warfare **12**, 57, 60–61, **60**, **61**, 73
Chi Feng-tian, Maj-Gen 52, 53, 76
Chiang Kai-shek 5, 26, 34, 36, 46, 54
  and Central Army 9, 16, 17, 41, 53, 55, 71
  and 'doomsday' plan 6, 56, **62**
  launches counter-attacks (1939) 75
  rise to power/extent of control 5, 7
  seeks ceasefire 74
China Garrison Army 5, 12, 14, 30, **31**, 38, 39, 70–71
  armour cos 38, 39
  artillery regt **31**, 48
  combined-arms regt 6
  corps **28**, 39, 70
  extent of presence in China 6
  infantry forces 6, **14**, **15**, 30, **31**, 33
  uniforms/clothing **14**, **15**, **29**
Chinese collaborators/traitors 25, 38, 40
Chongqing, as China's capital 55, 69, 74
Communist Chinese forces 23, 26, 49

De'an, fighting for 57, 58, 60

East Hebei Autonomous Government 5, 6, **7**
Peace Preservation Corps 30, 35, 40

Feng Zhi-an, Lt-Gen 34, 35, 76
Fengtai, forces in 6, 30, 33, 34, 35, 38, **38**

grenade dischargers 12, 21, 22
grenades: (Chi) **9**, **10**, 19, 35, 36, 37, 48, 49, 53, 58, 66; (Jpn) 21
Gu'an, Chinese forces retreat to 30, 40
Guangzhou campaign 56, 69, 74
Guoliji, fighting at 44, **45**, 53

Hanzhuang, fighting for 44, 52
Hashimoto Gun, Maj-Gen 33, 34, 36
Hata Shunroku, Gen 56, 77, 78
Hefei, fighting for 56, 57
HMG cos (Chi) 29, **43**
HMGs: (Chi) 18, 19, 29, 43, **43**; (Jpn) **20**, 22, 39, 40, 42
Homma Masaharu, Lt-Gen 58, 60, 78

Ichiki Kiyonao, Maj 29, 32, 33, 34
Imperial Japanese Army
  actions/influence of 'hawks' 6, 35–36, 42, 44, 70, 72–73, 74
  area of operations 25, 74
  air bdes/regts/sqns 12, 25, 36, 63
  armoured units 21: tank cos/regts 12, 62
  artillery forces 12, 17, 20, 26, 30, **31**, 34, 36, 42, 47, **47**, 48, 52, 53, 60, 61, 63
  brutality/cruelty of 25, 26, 27, 49, 62
  cavalry force 24, 25
  corps 6, 42–43, 44, **45**, 57, **59**, 71, 72
  garrisons 5, 6, 12, 36, 57
  independent mixed bdes **31**, 42
  infantry bdes 12, **31**, **45**, **59**, **64–65**, 66
  infantry dvns 5, 6, 12, 20, 24, 26, **31**, 36, 37, 41, 42, 43, 44, **45**, 46, 55, 56, **59**, 66
  infantry regts 12, 13, **31**, **45**, 54, 70
  machine-gun cos/pltns/teams **20**, 21, 22
  and martial/warrior spirit 12, 21, 27
  recruitment/training 12, 13, 24, 25, 72
  reservists 12, 13, 27, 60, 61, 62, 68
  rifle bns/pltns/squads 12, **12**, 21–22
  tactics/tactical philosophy 12, 19–21, 61
Imperial Japanese Navy 12, 25, **25**, 56, 57, 74
Isogai Rensuke, Lt-Gen 46, 47, 48, 49, 52, 53–54, 77
Itagaki Seishiro, Lt-Gen 46, 47, 52, 77
Ito Masaki, Lt-Gen 60, 69, 78

Jiaxiang, fighting for 44, **45**, 48
Jicha Political Council 5, 6, **7**
Jin Zhen-zhong, Lt-Col 28–29, 33, 34, 35
Jinan, fighting for 6, 43, 46, 47
Jiujiang, fighting for 57, 58, **59**, 62, 63
Ju County, fighting for 44, **45**, 47, 48

Katsuki Kiyoshi, Lt-Gen 38, 42–43, 46, 76
Kawabe Masakazu, Maj-Gen 30, 33, 34, 76
Kwantung Army (Manchuria)
  air force/sqns 5, 36
  armoured cos 34
  artillery bns/pltns 30, 34
  bdes: 38th 36
  hawks' behaviour 5–6, 19, 29, 37
  independent mixed bdes 5, 30, **31**, 36, 39–40
  infantry dvns 5, 30, **31**, 36, 38, 39, 40
  infantry regts 29, 30, **31**, 32, 33, 34, 36, 37, 38, 40
  machine-gun cos 29, 32, 33, 34
  rifle cos 29, 30, 32, 33
  tank pltns 33, 34

Langfang, fighting at 35, 36–37, 40
Leiminggu-liu, fighting at 58, **59**, 63, 66, 67–68, 69
Li Zong-ren, Gen (1st Grade) 46, 47, 48, 53, 72, 76, 77
Lin City, fighting for 44, 52, 53
Linyi, fighting for 47–48, 52, 53, 72
LMGs: (Chi) 18, **18**, 19, 61; (Jpn) **12**, **14**, 18, 21, **67**

Manchuria, annexation of 5, 6, 16, 27
Marco Polo Bridge Incident **10**, **11**, **14**, **15**, **18**, 19, 24, 28–30, **31**, 32–40, **32**, 43, 76
Matsuura Junrokuro, Lt-Gen 57, 58, 61, 62–63, 68, 78
mortar cos/teams: (Chi) 29, 34; (Jpn) **12**, **21**
mortars: (Chi) 29, 60; (Jpn) 21, 22, **22**, 38
Mutaguchi Renya, Col **29**, 32, 33, 34, 36, 37, 70, 76

Nagase Takehira, Maj-Gen 44, 48, 77
Nanjing, fighting for 6, 16–17, 18, 27, 41, 55, 57, 71, 74
Nanyuan, fighting for 30, 35, **37**, 38–40
National Army
  army groups 9, 17, 44, **45**, 46, 48, 49, 52, 53
  artillery bdes/dvns/regts 8, 17, 18, 30
  cavalry forces 8, 23, 36, 38, 40, 48
  corps **31**, 35, 38, 40, 44, **45**, 46, 47, 48, 58, **59**, 60, 61, 63, 71, 72
  deficiencies/weaknesses 8, 9, 16–18, 19, 21, 23–24, 26, 39, 40, 41, 43, 46, 48, 56, 71–72, 73
  fighting calibre/spirit 8–9, 19, 23, 26, 47, 52, 54, 72
  infantry bdes 8, 30, 36, 37, 40, **45**, 47, 48, 49, **50–51**, 52, 53, 63
  infantry dvns 8, 12, 26, 30, 34, 35, 36, 37, 40, 44, **45**, 47, 48, 49, 52, 53, 54, 58, **59**, 61, 62, 63, 69
  infantry regts 8, 29, 30, 34, 36, 37, **45**, 52, 53, 61, 63
  recruitment/training 7, 9, 10, 16, 17, 18, 19, 23, 24, 39, 40, 71, 72, 73, **77**
  regional forces 8, **9**, 17, **17**, 46–47, 48, **50–51**, 53, 54, 61, **67**, **68**, 72, **77**
  tactics/doctrine 9, 16, 17, 19, 24, 48, **64–65**, 66, 67, 73
  uniforms/clothing **5**, **10**, **11**, **27**, **77**, **79**
Nishio Toshizo, Lt-Gen 43, 44, 46, 77
North China Area Army **45**, 46, 55, 56
  armour cos 48, 52
  artillery bns/regts **45**, 47, 48, 52, 53
  corps **45**, 46, 55
  infantry bdes **45**, 47
  infantry dvns **45**, 46, 47, 48, 52, 53
  infantry regts **45**, 47, 48, 49, 52, 54

Ogisu Rippei, Lt-Gen 42, 46, 52, 77
Okamura Yasuji, Lt-Gen 56, 57, 60, 63, 68, 69, 72, 75, 78

Pang Bing-xun, Maj-Gen 47, 72, 76
pistols: (Chi) 17, **17**, 19, **64–65**; (Jpn) **12**, 15

rifles: (Chi) **9**, **10**, 19, 53, **61**, **64–65**, **67**, 72; (Jpn) **12**, 21, **21**, **38**, 63, 72
Ruichang, fighting for 58, 60

Saeda Yoshishige, Maj-Gen 58, 60, 63, 68, 78
Sakai Koji, Maj-Gen 30, 36, 40, 76
Sakamoto Jun, Maj-Gen 44, 47, 48, 53, 77
scimitars (Chi) **11**, **32**, 35, 49, **50–51**, **64–65**, 66, 67, **71**
Seya Hajime, Maj-Gen 44, 48, 49, 52, 53, 77
Shahe, fighting for 40, 58, **59**, 60
Shanghai, fighting for 5, 16–17, **17**, 18, 53, 54, 57, **61**
Song Zhe-yuan, Gen (2nd Grade) 6, 28, 34, 35, 36, 38, 71, 76
Sun Lian-zhong, Gen 9, 52, 76
Suzuki Harumatsu, Maj-Gen 58, 68, 78
Suzuki Shigeyasu, Lt-Gen 30, 36, 39–40, 76
swords: (Chi) **5**, 19, **27**; (Jpn) **27**, **64–65**

Tai'erzhuang, fighting for 6, 9, 16, 17, 24, 41–44, **45**, 46–49, 52–54, 72, 76–77
Tang En-bo, Lt-Gen 44, 48, 52, 53, 76, 77
Tashiro Kanichiro, Maj-Gen 33, 38, 76
Teng County, fighting for 44, **45**, 48–49, **50–51**, 52, 54
Tianjin, fighting for 6, **29**, 30, 34, 36, **39**, 40, 46, 71
Tuanhe, fighting for 30, 38

Wanjialing campaign 6, 16, 24, 55–58, **59**, 60–63, **64–65**, 66–69, 78
Wanping County, fighting for 28–29, 30, 32, 33, 34–35, 38, 40
warlord armies 4, 10, 16, 17, 26, 71
Wuhan campaign 6, 17, 25, 43, 52, 54, 55, 56–57, 60–61, **67**, 69, 72, 73, 75, 79

Xiamen/Xingzi, fighting for 56, 58, **59**, 60
Xiao-ao, forces around 58, **59**, 60
Xue Yue, Lt-Gen 57, 63, 68, 72, 75, 77
Xuzhou campaign 6, 43, 46, 47, 52, 54, 55